WIN AT SPADES

BASIC AND
INTERMEDIATE TECHNIQUES

Joseph D. Andrews

Bonus Books, Inc.
Chicago, Illinois

Cover design: Karen Sheets

"Bicycle", 808, the Ace of Spades, and "The United States Playing Card Company" trademarks are the sole property of The United States Playing Card Company and are used with permission.

Bonus Books, Inc.
160 East Illinois Street
Chicago, Illinois 60611

Library of Congress Cataloging-in-Publication Data
Andrews, Joseph D.
    Win at spades : basic and intermediate techniques / Joseph D. Andrews.
        p.   cm.
    ISBN 1–56625–117–6 (pbk.)
    1. Spades (Game) I. Title.
GV1295.S65A43   1999
795.4 — dc21   98–48840
                                                                    CIP

Published in the United States of America
1 2 3 4 5 6 — 04 03 02 01 00 99

*This book is dedicated to my niece, Laura Lee Dykes,
and to my nephew, Scott Brian McCready.*

*Special thanks to my dear and loving sister, Patricia Anne,
for all of her help with the editing and computer expertise
required to make this book a reality*

CONTENTS

PREFACE

Spades is a wonderful game, having descended from Whist and Bridge. It first appeared in the late 1930s, was popularized in the military during the 1940s, and soon after, spread to college campuses. It is now the #1 four-handed card game on the Internet. Spades is usually played as a partnership game; however, there is an Individual's variation for two or three persons. It is a deceptively easy game to learn — but don't let the simplicity of the rules fool you!

Partnership Spades provides a perfect setting for team competition, and the application of skill in interpreting the meaning of your opponent's bids and plays. You and your partner work together — bidding the optimum contracts, playing the hands cooperatively, and utilizing good defensive technique. Part of the game's fascination is the *nil bid* — in which the emphasis is on making *zero* tricks in a given hand. Another interesting feature is the *"bag rule,"* in which the unfortunate player who makes overtricks is penalized. Finally the *"set"* or defeat of the opponents' contract is punished by a reduction of their score.

This book will guide you through the rules and basic elements of the game. For those with some experience, you will sharpen your skills by reviewing the bidding strategy, tips for play of the hand, and defensive techniques. There is a section featuring the Internet and another chapter highlighting Duplicate Spades — a new game. The sequel to this book, *Advanced Play and Strategy* is the perfect continuation, and will provide an opportunity to move your game to an even higher level.

Perhaps someday, you will compete for a National Championship in a "live" event, or play against some of the "heavy hitters" on the Internet. *Have fun and enjoy the game!*

— Joseph Andrews, December 1998

PROLOGUE

The modern game of Spades became popular in the late 1940s, especially on college campuses. It is difficult to ascertain the true origin of this game. However, a review of several card game reference sources reveal that Spades is a descendant of Whist. Spades also has a kindred spirit with Bridge, Pinochle, Five Hundred and other similar games featuring partnership play, bidding, and a trump suit. George Coffin, the great Bridge author, traced the roots of Spades to the midwest. He determined that this game was introduced in Cincinnati sometime between 1937 and 1939. From there, it spread to other cities in the general region, and eventually into the military. Spades was played extensively during World War II, as it was a fast-paced game that could be interrupted at any time — especially during battle conditions.

In the olden days of Whist, some chap disliked having to turn his last card as dealer to determine trump. He would find it to be a singleton, while holding seven cards of another suit, perhaps, A K Q J XXX. To avoid such quirks of chance, this bright chap introduced the dealer's right to declare his best suit for trump. Later, another player conceived the idea of *bridging* to his partner the privilege to name trump. Next came Bid Whist, a competitive auction, and the option for a "declarer" to play the hand. However, Whist had been in a steady decline for several years. In 1925, the late Harold S. Vanderbilt created the game of Contract Bridge. The key feature of his innovation was the fact that you could not score game unless you had bid it. In addition, Vanderbilt

xii WIN AT SPADES

added special bonuses for successfully bid and made slams (12 or 13 tricks). Soon, Ely Culbertson created additional features that helped to make Bridge the outstanding game it is. Later, the innovation of the Duplicate format elevated Bridge to its highest level.

Canasta, a first rate card game, originated in South America and had become a fad in the early 1950s. As a matter of fact, the American Contract Bridge League (ACBL), was very concerned about the incredible growth of this new game, but the craze soon subsided, and by late 1954, Canasta was just about forgotten. In my opinion, Canasta is still a wonderful game with plenty of strategy. Bridge rebounded quite nicely, thanks to the many efforts of pioneers such as Oswald Jacoby, Samuel Stayman, Easley Blackwood, John Gerber, George Coffin and finally, Charles Goren. Most of today's Bridge conventions were named after their creators. However, it was Goren, a Philadelphia lawyer who was generally given credit for promoting Bridge. His POINT-COUNT BIDDING SYSTEM became the basis for what is now known as the STANDARD AMERICAN SYSTEM. This enabled novice players to learn the game quickly and comfortably.

Another trail blazer, Alfred Sheinwold, wrote a daily syndicated newspaper column and a classic Bridge book entitled FIVE WEEKS TO WINNING BRIDGE (1957). The ACBL enjoyed phenomenal growth into the 1970s. Today, Bridge still has a huge following of devotees and a wonderful network of dedicated directors.

Meanwhile, Spades continued its steady growth and established itself nationally. It is now the number one card game in colleges as well as in the military services. The appeal of Spades is the relatively basic bidding system, opportunity for partnership play, and the fast paced action. There is also a fertile ground for advanced techniques. Many Bridge players have "cut their eye teeth" on Spades before graduating to Bridge. Spades is also the most popular card game on the Internet, although some will argue a case for Poker and Blackjack. I do not consider the comparison to gambling card games as valid. Casino games of all types will always have a huge following of individuals who play against the odds established by the House. They also play for money. For the record, the most frequently played card game in the United States is Solitaire. The popularity of Spades is ensured as the Internet becomes more and more accessible. Eventually, a series of "live" tournaments and a national rating system will allow anyone to seek a competitive game — locally and regionally. For more information about the Internet sites, and the International Hearts and Spades Players' Association (IHSPA), please refer to the last chapter of this book.

Chapter One
A GLOSSARY OF TERMS

Italics denote definitions referenced in the Advanced Edition.

AUCTION — The interval in which the bidding occurs.

BAG(S) — Additional trick(s) over and above a specific bid (e.g., a bid of five making seven would yield two bags). Note — Each bag, per se, has no penalty value; however, an accumulation of ten bags is assessed a 100 point penalty.

BEMO — A bidding system which rewards a partnership for winning the first six tricks of a hand (plus 100 points).

BID — a number from 1–13 specifying a QUANTITY of tricks a player hopes to win in a given hand. Note — a bid of nil or blind nil is a declaration to take zero tricks. The opening bid is declared by the player to the dealer's immediate left.

BLIND NIL — A bid of zero which is made before a player sees his cards. Note — a successful blind nil bid scores plus 200 points. An unsuccessful blind nil bid scores minus 200 points. In some circles a

1

"pass" of one or two cards is exchanged after a blind nil bid. This is optional, and not recommended for competitive games.

BROKEN — Jargon for the playing of a spade (trump) which allows for subsequent leads of spades. Note — trumps cannot be led until a spade has been played or the player on lead has nothing but spades in his hand.

CASH — To play an established winning card (e.g., Ace of trump, or a winning card of another suit).

CONTRACT — The final combined partnership bid (e.g., North bids three, South bids five, yielding a contract of eight tricks for that partnership).

CONTROL — *A key high card* — *usually the established Ace or King of a suit.*

CONVENTION — *A partnership agreement denoting a specific meaning to a bid or discard.*

COVER (a) — A general term describing support of your partner's nil bid by playing key high cards or trumping strategically.

COVER (b) — The play of the next immediate high card of the suit led (e.g., your right hand opponent leads the Queen of diamonds; if you hold the King of diamonds, your play of this card is a "cover".)

CUTTHROAT — Another term for an individual's variation of the game where each person plays "solo" instead of partnership.

DEFENDER — (DEFENSE) — The term for the partnership which attempts to defeat or set their opponents' bid. Note — Each partnership has a dual function to **make** their own bid, and if possible, to defeat their opponents' bid.

DISCARD — The play of another suit when void of the suit led (instead of trumping).

DOUBLETON — A term for holding exactly two cards in any suit.

DRAW — Another word referring to the cashing of winners in the trump suit (spades).

DUCK — A strategic play of a low card usually intended to avoid **bags**.

DUPLICATION — *Equal values in the same suit distributed between a partnership (e.g., you hold in diamonds — Ace, Queen, 10, 7, 4; your partner holds in the same suit — King, Jack, 9, 6. The trick taking value here is significantly reduced as the opponents will probably **trump** on the second or third round.)*

ECHO — *A suit count signal which gives a partner a reading on the length of a specific suit which you hold (e.g., you hold the 8 and 4 of clubs. On the first round, you play the 8; on the second round, you play the 4 — this indicates to your partner that you hold a doubleton in clubs and can trump on the next lead.) This is sometimes called "a high-low signal".*

ENCOURAGE — *The play of a high card under your partner's high-card lead of the same suit which signals your partner to continue in that suit.*

ENDPLAY — *A strategic maneuver in which an opponent is thrown into the lead at the end of a hand and is forced to make a favorable return (to your hand).*

FOURS — *A bidding system requiring each player to bid four tricks. The total bid of 16 tricks results in a guaranteed set for at least one of the partnerships.*

ENTRY — Any card which allows access to a partner's hand.

FINESSE — An effort to win a trick with a card which is not the highest card in a given suit. (e.g., You hold the Ace and Queen of a suit while not on lead. That suit is led and you play the Queen hoping to win two tricks.)

GRAND SLAM — A successful contract of 13 tricks.

HOMICIDE — A bidding system in which the combined number of tricks must equal 14. This forces someone to be set or defeated.

HONOR — The Ace, King, Queen, Jack or 10 of any suit, often called **honor** cards.

HESITATION — An unethical or deceptive practice of intentionally delaying the play of a card in order to convey information to partner. Note — Another term for this is lagging and usually refers to the delay of playing a card while in a computer or Internet game.

HOLDUP — The intentional choice of ducking a trick that could have been won.

JOKER — A card or cards added to the deck in order to create a new variation. Jokers are ranked above the Ace of spades.

LEAD — The first card played to or after any trick or the first play of a hand. Note — In this book, the opening leader is the player to the right of the dealer. Another variation is the lead from the left of the dealer.

LHO/RHO/OAT — Abbreviations for Left Hand Opponent; Right Hand Opponent; and Opponent Across Table. Note — "OAT" is not applicable in this edition, as the player across from you is your Partner.

LITTLE — Non-honor cards (9, and below) often called "spot cards".

LIMIT — (GAME) — Usually 500 points for partnership or 300 points for individuals. Note — some rulebooks have a negative limit of minus 300 points. Another variation is a specified number of hands — usually 10 per round.

LONG — Holding great length in any suit (e.g., Ace, King, XXXX is referred to as "Ace, King, sixth"; "Ace, Queen, xx" is referred to as "Ace, Queen, fourth.") Note — Most of the combinations indicate the number of cards held in each suit.

MAJOR SUIT — spades and hearts

MAKE — A space term synonymous with the successful completion of a bid or contract (e.g., "Making" a bid of four tricks).

MINOR SUIT — clubs and diamonds

MIRROR — *A bidding system in which the actual number of spades in your hand denotes your bid.*

MOON — *(Grand Slam) — a bid to take all 13 tricks. Successful moon bids score a premium of 200 points. (Optional)*

NIL — A bid of zero in which a player expects to take no tricks. A successful nil bid scores a premium of 100 points. Blind nil is also a zero bid; however, the player cannot look at his/her cards prior to making this call.

OVERRUFF — A term for the playing of a higher trump on the same trick by the next person in rotation. (e.g., North leads the four of diamonds, the next player, East, is void in diamonds. East chooses to trump with the five of spades. South, the next player in turn, is also void in diamonds, and plays the six of spades. This is called "overruffing.")

OVERTRICK — Any trick or book in excess of a bid (e.g., a bid of four making five would have one "overtrick").

PASS — In some circles, as pass of one or two cards is made between the partners after a blind nil bid. This is strictly for a fun game only.

PENALTY — Points lost for failure to make any bid or contract; also, points deducted for the accumulation of bags in increments of ten.

REVOKE — Failure to follow suit whenever possible. In live games, the penalty for revoke is loss of bid. Internet or computer games do not allow revoking. Note — Another term for revoke is "renege."

RUFF — Another word for trumping.

RUFF/SLUFF — The lead of a suit in which both opponents are void. The result is usually a discard by one opponent as the other trumps. This is considered a very poor play.

SECOND HAND LOW — The practice of playing a low card in the second position after the lead. This allows partner a chance to win the trick in fourth position.

SET — The taking of less tricks than the number specified or the defeating of the opponents contract. (Synonymous with "defeat.")

SMALL SLAM — A bid of 12 tricks. If successful, the premium is 100 points. (Optional)

SEQUENCE — Connected honor cards of the same suit in the same hand. (e.g., King, Queen, Jack; or Ace, King, Queen; or, Queen, Jack, 10, etc.)

SINGLETON — The holding of only one card in a suit.

SQUEEZE — A forced play against an opponent who must guard two or more suits simultaneously, and thus is forced to discard a key card.

SUICIDE — A bidding system in which one member of a partnership is required to bid nil in every hand.

TABLE TALK — Jargon for any conversation about specific cards in one's hand or the meaning of a bid. This practice is both unethical and illegal.

TAKE — A term for winning or capturing a trick.

THIRD HAND HIGH — The standard play of your highest card in the third position in order to prevent the fourth player from winning a trick with a low card.

TRICK — Another word for a "book" or "packet" of four cards. There are 13 tricks in every hand.

TRUMP — The highest ranking suit which is always spades. This term is also applied to the play of a spade.

UNDERLEAD — The intentional lead of a low card from a suit containing one or more higher cards.

UNDERRUFF — The intentional play of a lower trump under a higher trump on the same trick (e.g., North leads the seven of hearts. East is void of hearts, and trumps with the ten of spades. South, also void in hearts, chooses to play the eight of spades. His play is an example of an "underruff.")

VOID — Holding no cards in a given suit.

Chapter Two

BASIC ELEMENTS

The basic rules and principles of Spades are relatively simple. Please refer to the next chapter if you are familiar with these bare essentials. Spades is in the same family of card games as Whist, Bridge and Pinochle.

THE PLAYERS

The standard game is four-handed with two sets of partnerships playing opposite each other. There is also a three-handed variation in which each person plays individually. Finally, a four-handed option exists with each person playing individually — although this form of the game is relatively obsolete. Although each person in the individual games plays for himself, two or more players may team up as a temporary partnership if this is advantageous for them. Note — the individuals' games are reviewed and analyzed in the book — *Win at Spades: Advanced Play and Strategy.*

THE PACK

A standard 52-card deck is used. There are four suits and the cards of each suit rank as follows:

Ace (high), King, Queen, Jack, ten, nine and so forth down to the deuce.

Spades are always trump and outrank the other three suits. The terms major and minor are used for quick identification only. Major suits are hearts and spades; minor suits are diamonds and clubs. The Ace, King, Queen, Jack and ten are called "honor" cards; the deuce to the nine are called "spot" cards.

THE OBJECT OF THE GAME

Each partnership strives to win the highest score which is usually 500 points. This is accomplished by capturing tricks, setting or defeating the opponent's **contracts** and avoiding the accumulation of overtricks. The **standard** game limit for partnership variation is 500 points. Individual games have a limit of 300 points. There are penalties for defeated contracts, as well as the accumulation of overtricks (bags). In tournament play, the game limit is ten hands. This is designed to control the time, as well as length of each round.

SCORING

Each successful **contract** scores 10 points for every trick bid and made as well as one point for every additional trick. For example, if you bid seven (combined partnership) and make nine (tricks) you score 70+2 for a total of 72 points. If you are unsuccessful in making your bid (**set**) your team loses 10 points for every trick bid. Using the above example, if your team was defeated in the contract of seven tricks the result would be minus 70 points.

Remember, partnership bids are *combined* and the total made or set is the basis of the scoring. Successful **nil bids** score a premium of 100 points. Defeated nil bids have a penalty of minus 100 points. Please note that a nil is an *individual* contract and the partner of the nil bidder has his or her score calculated **separately**. For example; if I bid nil and my partner bids three and we are both successful, we score plus 130 points. If my partner is set and I still make my nil bid, we score plus 70 (100 minus 30). Any tricks taken by a nil bidder do **not** count toward the total of the other partner's bid. Successful **blind nils** have a premium of 200 points, and a defeated blind nil is penalized 200 points.

BAGS (SANDBAGS)

Bags are a penalty for over-conservative bidding. Every additional trick (overtrick) in a successful contract counts as one bag. An accumulation of 10 bags results in a penalty of 100 points. It is quite possible to "sit" on a total of nine bags and not incur a penalty. Bags are sometimes called "Sandbags."

Chapter Three

GETTING STARTED

As stated previously the most frequently played variety of spades is **partnership.** The first step is to draw cards for partners unless you already have a partner. The two players who have drawn the two highest cards are partners against the other two. In the event of a tie, the suits are ranked spades, hearts, diamonds and then clubs, as in the game of Bridge. The King of hearts is higher than the King of clubs, etc. Note that the ranking of suits has relevance only in this instance. Each player sits at a specific direction opposite his or her partner. This book will always use the layout shown here.

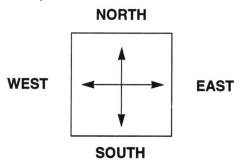

Both pairs are "teams" and compete as partnerships (North/South vs. East/West). Two decks of cards are recommended for each table. One deck is in use and the other is prepared for the next deal. If only one deck is available that is quite acceptable. The dealer is determined by a draw of cards or mutual agreement. The deck is thoroughly shuffled and then offered to the player on the dealer's immediate right for the "cut" — which may be declined. The cards are then dealt one at a time, in a clockwise rotation until the whole deck is depleted. Each person thus receives 13 cards. It is always a good idea to count your cards ensuring a proper deal. Any misdeal is "thrown in," and the hand is re-dealt after a new shuffle and cut.

SORTING YOUR HAND

At this point, each player sorts his or her cards in a logical fashion.

This is best accomplished by **alternating** the colored suits starting with diamonds, then clubs, hearts and finally spades on the right of your hand. The ranking of cards in each suit should be from highest to lowest. This will enable you to identify you suits and key cards more quickly. Nothing is more confusing than to have your hand sorted in a haphazard fashion which could result in a **renege** or incorrectly played card.

Here are some typical sorted hands from left to right:

$\diamondsuit$ A 5 3 $\clubsuit$ 10 9 7 2 $\heartsuit$ K 3 2 $\spadesuit$ J 9 6

Here is another example featuring a **void** suit:

$\diamondsuit$ K Q J 5 3 $\spadesuit$ A 7 6 5 2 $\heartsuit$ Q 9 5

Note that the **spades** are placed on the **far right**, if possible, or in the middle with a void in clubs and two red suits. If void in a red suit, then start with clubs on the far left, the other red suit, and then spades. If you follow this basic plan, you will be able to proceed with your bid and play your hand more comfortably.

TRICKS (BOOKS)

The play of every deal consists of 13 tricks. Each trick is a packet or book containing four cards — one from each players' hand. Cards are played individually in a clockwise rotation and placed face up on the table. Remember, each player must follow in turn. For example, if East leads a card, South then plays next, followed by West, and finally North.

BRIEF OVERVIEW

There are three basic phases to every hand of Spades — **the bidding, the play, and the scoring.** There is a specific rotation of play in which each player follows a precise clockwise pattern. However, before we discuss bidding, it is necessary to understand the play first. After the deal and bidding sequence is completed, the opening leader (**the person seated to the immediate right of the dealer**) plays the first card of the hand. Trump may **not** be led until spades have been played ("**broken**") or that player has nothing left in his hand but spades. The examples illustrated below will establish a pattern for the way each trick is played.

OPENING LEAD / ROTATION OF PLAY

The player making the opening lead is seated to the **right of the dealer.** Some groups allow the dealer to make the opening lead, still others follow the pattern of Bridge which requires that the opening lead be made to the left of the dealer. Another variation is the "deuce of clubs" lead. The player who holds the club deuce must lead this card to start the play of the first trick. The winner of this trick (usually the highest club unless it is ruffed) now leads the first card of the second trick. For our purposes we will adhere to the following:

The opening bid is made by the player to the left of the dealer and the opening lead is made by the player to the right of the dealer. The logic for this is the sharing of responsibilities by two different players, rather than giving the opening bidder an additional advantage of having the first lead. The opening leader selects any card other than spades, and places it face up on the table. Then, in rotation, each player follows suit if possible, and the highest card of the suit led wins that trick. For example:

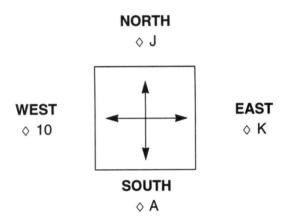

NORTH
◇ J

WEST
◇ 10

EAST
◇ K

SOUTH
◇ A

East is the dealer and the bidding has been completed. North makes the opening lead of the Jack of diamonds. East plays the King; South covers with his Ace and West plays his 10.

Note the clockwise rotation and the following play of cards in the same suit. South wins this trick, forms a book of four cards and places it face down on the table. Now South having won the last trick, makes the opening lead to the next trick. Each player must follow suit if they can. If a player cannot follow the suit led, then he can either discard another suit, or trump with a spade. Here is another example:

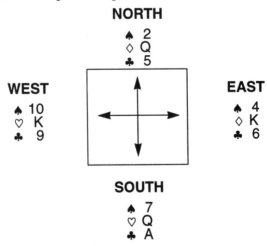

NORTH
♠ 2
◇ Q
♣ 5

WEST
♠ 10
♡ K
♣ 9

EAST
♠ 4
◇ K
♣ 6

SOUTH
♠ 7
♡ Q
♣ A

North leads the Queen of diamonds, East covers with the King, and now South has a choice. He may discard the Queen of hearts or the Ace of clubs, or may trump with his singleton spade.

Note that the Ace of clubs if discarded, does not win the trick as it is a neutral card. If South chooses not to trump, West has the option to allow his partner to win the trick with the King of diamonds. If South does choose to trump this trick, then West, who is also void of diamonds, may overruff with his spade 10. Another option for West is to make a discard of a heart or club and allow South to take the trick. Remember diamonds were played initially. This allows many options for West and South whereas East has no choice but to follow suit.

Spades (trump) is the key element of the game. Any trump, even the lowly deuce, ranks higher than any card of any other suit. If you are void of hearts and you hold the deuce of spades, you have a winner should you choose to trump (and the other two players have to follow suit). When a trick contains **two or more trump**, it is won by the person who plays the **higher or highest trump**. This applies to both the lead of trump or the use of trump to ruff a side suit.

Assume that we are at the end of the hand and these are the last two tricks. North is on lead and chooses to play the four of spades, East must play the three, South follows with the ten, and West wins with the

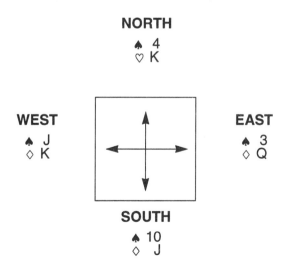

NORTH

♠ 4
♡ K

WEST

♠ J
◊ K

EAST

♠ 3
◊ Q

SOUTH

♠ 10
◊ J

Jack. This is straightforward and now West will win the last trick with the King of diamonds. Now let us suppose North selects the lead of the King of hearts. This changes the matrix. East may try for a spade ruff (rather than the diamond discard) and South may be tempted to over-ruff with the spade 10. West, also void in hearts, wins the Jack. He must then concede a trick to North's last trump. Had North chosen to lead his spade first, West would have taken two tricks. The heart lead by North allows the establishing of the spade four by having his partner force the Jack of spades with his ten. This is a theme which will be ana-lyzed more thoroughly in the advanced Spades book. Trump promo-tion is a somewhat advanced technique. In Bridge books, it is called "uppercutting." Often, it will spell the difference between a successful contract or a set contract.

Chapter Four
BIDDING

Bidding is the most important part of the game. No matter how well you are able to play hands, the wrong bid can lead to a lot of problems. Each partnership strives to meet the **optimum contract**. The player to the immediate left of the dealer is designated as the first bidder, and then each of the other players bid in turn, clockwise. Unlike bridge, there is only **one round** of bidding in the game of spades. This is why it is absolutely essential to listen closely to any bids which may precede yours — **especially your partner's bid.** In Spades, the only acceptable bids are the numbers 1 to 13, or a bid of zero which is called "nil" or "blind nil." ("Zero" is never actually bid, instead the word "nil" is used.) The basis of a bid is the number of tricks a player **expects** to take. For example if a player holds two Aces in side suits, and the King, Queen, and one small spade — a bid of three is quite reasonable. However, a bid of four is probably a bit aggressive in that the player may not be able to take two spade tricks unless his or her partner holds the Ace of spades. Another chance for an additional spade trick exists if the Ace of spades is held by the right-hand opponent. Suit names and the words "no trump" are never mentioned during the bidding and each player is allowed only **one bid per hand.** There is no call of "Pass" during the round of bidding: therefore, the minimum numerical bid is one or a bid of nil. It is quite possible that the total number of tricks bid may exceed 13. This situation would doom one of the partnerships to defeat. The fourth bid of each auction completes the round of bidding for that hand.

EVALUATING YOUR HAND

In order to bid properly, you must be able to accurately assess the number of tricks you expect to take. Other factors which may influence your bidding are: (a) **the position of your turn to bid**; (b) **your partner's bid**, (c) **the opponent's bids**, and finally, (d) **the score at that time.** In Spades, you are rewarded with more points if you bid aggressively: however, if you are set or defeated — you stand to lose more than if you had bid less aggressively. Basically, the **higher** you bid, the **higher** the risk. It is important to understand the scoring situation at the time of your bid and the trick-taking potential of certain card combinations. It is interesting to note that the bidding system in Spades is geared toward the conservative approach. There is a spatial relationship of the math and the result of making and losing contracts. For example, at the beginning of the game, each side starts out with zero points. If your partnership has a combined bid of 70 and you are set, your score becomes minus 70 points. If you make your contract your score is plus 70 points. In other words, there is a **swing** of 140 points here. It is probably best to bid one trick lower if there is any doubt as to the possibility of making your contract. This applies to card combinations which are borderline or dubious. Hand evaluation and bidding techniques are reviewed in a later chapter. A great concern is the **duplication of values** in the same suit between you and your partner. The following card combinations are listed as a guide to help you gauge the value of your hand. It is reasonable to assume that an Ace will usually be worth one trick. Of course, the Ace of spades is a guaranteed winner. Aces in side suits will usually win tricks as well. However, the longer a suit is, the less likely an Ace or for that measure, any high card, will win a trick. Kings are a very "iffy" proposition. If you hold a singleton King, the odds are very much against you. Either the opponents' Ace will drop your King, or your partner may prematurely play the Ace of that suit and swallow up your King. Thus, I rate a singleton King as somewhat limited and less than full value (though, as a face card, it does have some intrinsic qualities). The only instances where a singleton King has any worth (other than its distributional feature), occur when your partner holds the Ace or Queen of that suit, and does not play either card prematurely. Should you hold the King of a suit with two or three accompanying small cards, you have approximately a 50% chance of scoring your King if the opponents hold the Ace, and a much higher chance if your partner holds the Ace. If playing in a four-player individuals' game, the odds are greatly reduced. If your King is accompanied by more than three small cards, the chances of scoring a trick are greatly reduced. The only exception is the King of spades, which often becomes promoted when other high spades are played, or can be used to trump another suit. Queens are even more tenuous. A singleton queen is basically worthless and has value as any other low card singleton. A weak case can be argued for the use of a singleton Queen to help "cover" a nil bid, or to drive out an Ace or King. That is an example of stretching the limits. A Queen with one or two small spot cards is also shaky unless a partner holds the Ace or King. With the exception of the Queen of trump, the value of Queens in general, is speculative at best. Evaluating Jacks is a waste of time unless we are talking about the trump suit, and even then, the Jack requires at least two or three accompanying spot cards to be of any value. Even Queen-Jack sequences have a deflated quality — unless you have these cards in the trump suit. It is safe to conclude that **distribution** (singletons and voids) is of tremendous value. For if you are short in any suit, other than spades, you have the potential of "trumping in" for tricks when your short suit is led. The ideal holding is the singleton Ace of clubs, hearts or diamonds. Once you clear the Ace out of the way, you will be able to trump on the next lead of that suit.

Now we will cover what is called honor card combinations or **sequences** in the side suits (clubs, hearts, and diamonds). The accumulation of honor cards in the same suit greatly strengthens that suit. The Ace, King of the same suit will usually score two tricks unless there is great length in that suit. The King and Queen and one or two small cards in the same suit will score two tricks approximately 50 percent of the time unless your partner holds the Ace. Even then, it is a bit unrealistic to expect to take three tricks in the same suit, as the odds favor an opponent trumping on the third round. The Ace and Queen of the same suit will score two tricks 50 percent of the time with the help of a **finesse** (see chapter ten). Honor card combinations in the trump suit are valued much higher as their trick taking potential is greatly increased. Honor cards lose quite a bit of their potency if they are scattered among three or four suits.

PARTNER'S BID

Exactly fifty percent of the time, your partner's bid will precede yours. Occasionally he will have the opening bid or the second bid and your evaluation of your hand will be affected by his bid. The higher your partner bids, the less likely some of your high cards will score tricks. This is due to that old "sea dog" — **duplication!** This is especially true in the side suits. The greatest fear in any contract is that you and your partner will have **wasted values** — that is, an accumulation of high cards in the same suit. Furthermore, if your partner bids a nil or a low level numerical bid such as one or two, your hand may actually decrease in value. (He will not be able to promote your middle cards.) It really depends on the **cards you actually hold.** Finally, it is useful to note that if either opponent bids a **nil,** you may be forced to take additional tricks, especially if you are trying to set the nil. The ideal bidding seat is fourth position. In this case, you have the opportunity to listen to the other three bids preceding yours and then make your assessment of your hand accordingly.

BAGS (PURPOSE AND STRATEGY)

Bags, or sandbags, are a part of the game which affects scoring. The purpose of bags is to punish overly conservative bidders and to offset the occasional inequities of the luck of the deal. Without bags, the game is very dull and the bidding is very conservative. Each bag up to nine does not count as anything, however, **an accumulation of 10 bags** results in a **penalty of 100 points.** The real strategy of the game is the balance between accumulating bags and making your bids. There are players who go blithely about their way, gathering bags as if they did not have a care in the world. After a few score reductions of one hundred points at a time, their partners become frustrated and usually resolve the matter. There is also a determination which needs to be made for the value of setting the opponent's contract versus the number of bags required to accomplish this objective. We will cover this topic in greater detail later on in this book.

NIL (REFER TO CHAPTER SIX FOR MORE INFORMATION)

The bid of nil has a certain degree of risk. Unless you are fortunate to have a hand with all low cards and fewer than three small spades, you do have the threat of being set. The loss of 100 points is a very steep penalty for the defeated nil. The carnage is even worse for the set of a **blind nil** — a whopping 200 points! There are many fine players who effortlessly defeat many nils working cooperatively with their partner. The making of a nil bid is truly a **team** effort, as your partner will protect you — even at the risk of **losing** his or her bid! When you determine if a hand is worth bidding nil, the important thing to note is the **length and strength of your spade suit** as well as the number of unprotected high cards in your side suits. As for blind nil or double nil, this bid is best used when you are losing by a ton of points and must resort to desperation in order to have any hope of stealing a win. Anyone who makes an opening bid of blind nil for the first hand of a game should be marched off to the dunking tank, and immersed at least 20 times. The risk is just too great, and to start out a fresh game with a 200 point deficit is very unfair to your partner. Should you make a game-opening blind nil bid, you will incur the wrath of your opponents, who may very well counter with a blind nil bid of their own. Then the contest will be reduced to an exercise of nil bids, and random luck. For the record, a lot of players will not allow blind nil bids to be part of the rules. Remember, the bidder of a blind nil cannot look at his/her cards, and thus is at the mercy of the random luck factor.

Chapter Five

MORE ON BIDDING — NUMERICAL (1-13) BIDS

EVALUATION OF CARD COMBINATIONS

Please review these card combinations and numbers of *projected tricks.* "X" denotes a spot card (deuce through nine).

Percentage probabilities in the game of Spades are NOT equivalent to those in the game of Bridge. Spades partnerships consist of two individuals participating as a "team." The partnership aspect of Bridge is much different, as there is a "dummy" hand, only one person (the "declarer") actually playing the hand for his side. However, there is a somewhat parallel comparison, and a lot of the standard mathematical tables for Bridge can be used a guideline. (Some of the percentages are identical). The numbers listed below are adjusted for Spades.

I.   SIDE SUITS (HEARTS, DIAMONDS AND CLUBS).
    A.   Aces (denoted by "A"),
        1.   A (singleton) — one trick
        2.   A x (doubleton) — one trick

25

3. A x x (Ace third) — one trick
4. A x x x (Ace fourth) **speculative** — will win one trick approximately 90% of the time. Remember, long suits have a risk factor!
5. A x x x x (Ace fifth or longer) **speculative** — will win one trick approximately 70 percent of the time, barring extreme length.

B. **Kings (denoted by "K")**. Note: The location of the Ace is very critical with various King holdings.
1. K (singleton) — **speculative** — should not win a trick unless partner holds the Ace or the opponents choose to duck.
2. K x (doubleton) — **speculative** — will win a trick approximately 50 percent of the time
3. K x x (King third) — **speculative** — will win a trick approximately 50 percent of the time
4. K x x x (King fourth) — **speculative** — will win a trick less than 40 percent of the time.
5. K x x x x (King fifth or longer) — **very speculative** and probably will not win a trick.

C. **Queens (denoted by "Q")** Note: The location of the Ace and/or King is very critical to Queen holdings.
1. Q (singleton) — **very speculative** — will probably not win a trick — partner must hold A K, and duck first round. (The opponents, however, may allow a singleton Queen to win a trick!)
2. Q x (doubleton) — **speculative** — will win a trick approximately 33 percent of the time.
3. Q x x (Queen third) — **speculative** — will win a trick approximately 40 percent of the time.
4. Q x x x and all other holdings — **very speculative** and probably will not win a trick.

D. **Ace-King combinations** Note: The trick taking power of Ace, King holdings is very dependent of length of partner's suit.
1. A-K (doubleton) — should win two tricks more than 98 percent of the time.

2. A-K x (third) — should win two tricks approximately 85 percent of the time.

3. A-K x x (fourth) should win two tricks approximately 50 percent of the time; and one trick approximately 90 percent of the time.

4. A-K x x x (fifth) — should win two tricks approximately 33 percent of the time; and one trick approximately 70 percent of the time.

5. A-K x x x x (or longer) — **speculative** — may win only one trick less than 25 percent of the time; two tricks is a longshot.

E. **Ace-Queen combinations** (Note: these are usually "finessing" situations)

1. A-Q (doubleton) — will win one trick more than 99 percent of the time and two tricks (depending on location of the King) 50 percent of the time.

2. A-Q x (third) — will win one trick more than 95 percent of the time and may win two tricks depending on location of the King.

3. A-Q x x (fourth) — will win one trick 90 percent of the time and may win two tricks depending on location of the King.

4. A-Q x x x — will win one trick 70 percent of the time and may win two tricks depending on location of the King; however the Ace should be taken on the first round. Note: The risk here is that the finesse will lose, and then the Ace will be ruffed on the second round.

5. A-Q x x x x (and longer) — will win one trick approximately 30 percent of the time; two tricks are virtually out of the question.

F. **King-Queen combinations**

1. K-Q (doubleton) — will win one trick more than 98 percent of the time and should win two tricks if partner holds the Ace and does not take it (an example of "duplication").

2. K-Q x (third) — will win one trick more than 80 percent of the time and may win two tricks depending on location of the Ace.

3. K-Q x x (fourth) — will win one trick 70 percent of the time and probably will not take two tricks unless partner holds the Ace with fewer than two other cards of the same suit.

4. K-Q x x x — will win one trick approximately 50 percent of the time, two tricks become **very speculative**.

5. K-Q x x x x (and longer) — will win one trick approximately 25 percent of the time, two tricks are virtually out of the question.

G. **King-Queen-Jack combinations**

1. K-Q — J (three cards only) — will win one trick more than 95 percent of the time; two tricks approximately 70 percent of the time and three tricks only if partner has the Ace and does not take it initially. (Three tricks are a very remote probability).

2. K-Q-J x (four cards only) — will win one trick approximately 90 percent of the time and may win two tricks approximately 50 percent of the time. Three tricks is out of the question unless there is a very unusual distribution of the suit.

3. K-Q-J x x (or longer) — will win one trick approximately 66 percent of the time. Two or more tricks are very speculative with this combination.

II **DISTRIBUTION VALUES (SIDE SUITS) (Distribution Values do not apply to the trump suit)**
Distributional features are essential to the evaluation of every hand.

1. **Voids** are valuable as they provide the ability to trump or discard on the first round of a missing suit. This is often called first-round control.

2. **Singletons** are useful as they allow the ability to trump or discard on the second round of the suit. A singleton Ace is golden and worth full value as one trick plus the clearing of that suit for second-round trumping.
3. **Doubletons** in a suit are helpful, but somewhat limited. A doubleton Ace is quite nice, for it allows the clearing of a suit in two rounds. Other doubletons can also be helpful especially when promoting trump tricks for partner.
4. **Three card holdings** in the same suit are virtually useless for distribution, as it is unrealistic to expect to win a ruff on the fourth round.

III   THE TRUMP SUIT (SPADES)
Unlike side suits, high trumps are as good as money in the bank. For there is no way to trump a trump. Here is a list of the trick-taking potential of various spade combinations:
1. Ace (singleton) — one trick (Obviously!).
2. A x or A x x — one trick.
3. A x x x — one trick; possibly two tricks if partner has length or the spot card is high and promotes to a trick.
4. King (singleton) — **speculative** — if partner has Ace, you SHOULD win your King. If opponents have Ace, you MAY win the King.
5. K x or K x x — **speculative** — will win a trick approximately 50 percent of the time depending on location of the Ace.
6. Queen (singleton) — **speculative** — will win a trick less than 25 percent of the time. Note: If partner has King, the Queen has value by driving out the opponent's Ace. She is also helpful if partner has the Ace-Jack combination, as the enemy King will be forced — setting up the Jack.

7. Q x or Q x x — speculative — will win a trick approximately 50 percent of the time depending on location and holder of the Ace –King.

8. Ace-King (doubleton) — two tricks!!

9. Ace-Queen (doubleton) — will win two tricks approximately 50 percent of the time depending on location of the King.

10. King-Queen (doubleton) — will win two tricks approximately 33 percent of the time depending on location of the Ace (Partner will have it one out of three times).

11. K-Q x or K-Q x x — will win two tricks approximately 50 percent of the time depending on location of the Ace.

12. A-J x or A-J x x — will win two tricks approximately 33 percent of the time depending on location of the King and/or Queen.

13. A-Q-J or A-Q-J x — will win 3 three tricks approximately 50 percent of the time depending on location of the King. The additional spot cards increase probability of the third trick.

14. K-Q-J — will win a guaranteed two tricks and a possible third trick if partner holds the Ace and at least three other spot cards.

15. Q-J-10 — will win one trick; two tricks if partner holds King.

16. Q-J x x — will win one trick approximately 70 percent of the time and two tricks if partner holds Ace or King.

17. J-10 x or J-10 x x — will win one trick approximately 50 percent of the time if the partner holds at least one higher honor card. Combinations such as these become very speculative based on lengths of suits in both hands.

18. Xxxxx (five spot cards) — should win at least one trick and possibly more if the suit if evenly divided. If you find yourself in a desperation nil bid with four or

five small trumps, there may still be salvation — if you can UNDERRUFF spades played by the opponents (or partner).

Please note that all trump combinations are very dependent on the distribution and location of key cards in the Spades suit. Another critical factor is the sequence of plays by the opponents. The trump suit is always a premium feature of any hand.

Chapter Six

BIDDING NIL

EVALUATING YOUR HAND/LOGICAL APPROACH

I — BIDS OF NIL

A successful nil bid is handsomely rewarded, and there are times when nil bidding is the only hope to salvage a lost game. Most nil bids have a risk factor. Some are downright ludicrous. A supportive partner who can protect your nil is a great asset. No matter how you slice it and dice it — you still must have the cards! There are some nils which are quite solid, and others which fall into the borderline category. The time has come to review a few of the potential "underbellies" (weaknesses that can croak nils)!

High spade holdings can be very dangerous. Trump honor cards in your hand are the equivalent of icebergs in the northern Atlantic in April of 1912. If you hold the Ace of spades, (especially after a blind nil bid) — you are sailing on the Titanic! The spade King is also shaky and requires that your partner holds the Ace — a rather big order. The spade Queen or Jack are nuisances that can be alleviated by the presence of the

Ace or King in your partner's hand or a very lucky lie of the cards — another ambitious request! Then again, there those opponents who are very hasty with the play of high spades which might allow you to dump a dangerous trump. Don't count on it in a game with seasoned opponents. Other explosive spade holdings are multiple high honor sequences such as K J x ; Q 9 x , J 10 x x; Q J x, etc. Most of these will usually advance you to one trump trick and sink a lot of nil bids. Resourceful and clever opponents can also force or steer a player with a weak trump holding into a hopeless situation.

Holdings of **middle spades** can also be very risky — unless you have two or less. For example: 10 9 8 or 10 x x x or J 9 x x can be a lot of trouble; however, 10 4 2 is good. Low spades are a premium unless you hold great length. Any four-card spade suit is suspect and a five "bagger" is big trouble — as a "long spade" may result in a trick. The only alternative with a long spade holding is to **underruff** (discard your spades under higher spades used in trumping). The greatest fear in holding trump of three or four card lengths while contemplating nil, is the risk of the opponents **cross ruffing** with their trumps. This results in the establishing of a spade winner in your hand — especially if one of your trumps is a Jack or Queen. I have seen instances where two small trumps in the nil bidder's hand were set up after the opponents took all of their trumps separately — an extraordinary result!

To determine the soundness of a nil, you must evaluate the quality of your **side suits** as well. Isolated high cards are a real problem and a concentration of high cards without accompanying low cards in the same suit is deadly. It reminds me of the game of Hearts in which the Queen of spades is the critical card. If you hold the dreaded Lady without sufficient "backers" or support cards, she will be drilled right out of your hand by repeated spade leads. Two or three key low cards (in the same suit of course) are usually safe, and a combination of low and high cards is also quite acceptable. It often boils down to which low cards you hold, the texture of the suits in question, and the overall quality of your hand. Remember, high cards are not the threat — it is the **lack of low cards in the same suit** that can determine the outcome. Here is a guideline of combinations in the side suits which you may use to gauge the feasibility of a nil bid. Please note that the next section of this chapter will review your partner's bid, which is often a deciding factor.

NIL BIDDING GUIDELINES —
CLUB, DIAMOND, AND HEART SUITS

COMBINATION (ONE SUIT)	EVALUATION
1. A Q 8	Very bad
2. A Q 8 5	Speculative/not recommended
3. A Q 8 5 2	Good
4. A Q 8 5 4 2	Fabulous!
5. K J 9	Very bad
6. K 9 3	Speculative and risky
7. K 9 5 3	Reasonable and worth a try
8. K 9 6 3 2	Marvelous!
9. K J 10	Horrible
10. Q J 10	Very bad/asking for trouble
11. Q J 7 6	Speculative and risky
12. Q J 6 3	Borderline, but quite reasonable
13. Q J 6 4 2	Safe
14. J 10 9	Begging for trouble
15. J 9 5	Speculative — but close!
16. J 9 4 2	Safe
17. Singleton K	Off the wall — Do you expect your partner to have the Ace?

18.	Singleton Q	Slightly better than the singleton King — but NOT MUCH BETTER
19.	Singleton J	Speculative, but worthwhile especially if your partner has bid at least three or higher
20.	Singleton A	Give me a break!!!!!

Note — If you have more than ONE weak side suit, do not bid nil, unless it is your only chance to salvage a lost game — or your partner has bid at least eight tricks!

Your opponent's bids are also a factor. If you are in fourth position and the opponents have a combined bid of eight tricks or more, a borderline nil hand becomes more attractive; however, if you have an obvious trump loser as well as a suspect side suit, you may be willing to reconsider your nil bid. Still — another outlet for getting rid of side suit losers is a void or singleton in another side suit. It is a bit thin, to be sure — but better than nothing. Another obvious question is: **Are the opponents willing to scuttle their own contract in order to set your nil?** In addition, they must consider the risk of accumulating bags in the process of attacking the nil. This is all dependent on the score at the time. If your opponents are bidding a total of less than five tricks, then you need much more overall quality (especially low cards) in order to bid nil. Finally your partner's bid (if you are in the fortunate position of having your partner bid **before** you) can quickly determine your chances of a successful nil. Remember, the higher your partner bids, the higher the probability that he or she will be able to protect your nil bid. If your partner bids less than four, you realistically cannot expect help (covering), and your hand must stand on its own. A four or five bid from a partner offers a modicum amount of support and a higher bid may be enough to send you on your way even with a shaky side suit. Never assume that a partner can screen you from a potential losing card — just because he or she bid a three or four. Then again, most nils are mild to moderate gambles, and appealing to a Higher Authority may be the only alternative!

If you are contemplating nil and have the first bid, you are pretty much on your own. If you are bidding in second position and your right hand opponent opens with five or higher, your borderline nil bid now becomes more attractive. If you have the first bid of a hand, and your potential nil bid is very shaky, it is best to play it safe and bid a low number rather than risk a set on a high degree of speculation. This too, will be dependent on the score at the time.

BIDDING SUMMARY — STANDARD (1-13) NON-NIL BIDS

1. **Distribution** is a critical factor in every hand. Voids and singletons (spot cards) are a plus.

2. A high bid by anyone (especially partner) tends to de-value your hand. Consider bidding one less trick unless your hand holds a precise number of guaranteed tricks (usually in the trump suit).

3. **Protected honor cards** in the **trump** suit are important. Furthermore, **spade length** is a tremendous asset, especially if you are void in a side suit.

4. A sure bet is an Ace or protected King. In trump, they are "naturals." Good bets are **honor sequences** in the same suit (e.g., A-K; K-Q-J; A-Q-J, etc.) Note: excessive length weakens the value of high cards.

5. Poor bets are singleton high spades except for the Ace, scattered honor cards in different suits, and very long side suits. Do not over-value Queens and Jacks, as these cards are really hard-pressed to win tricks.

BIDDING SUMMARY — NIL BIDS (ONLY)

6. Nils are sound bids if you have the right card combinations and minimal trump risk. A high bid by your partner that precedes your nil bid is very reassuring.

7. Your partner is your best friend — but you cannot assume that he or she will always have the key cards which you may need (for protecting your nil).

8. If your partner has bid a nil preceding your bid, and your hand has nil potential — forget about it! No matter how nice your hand, two

opposite nils are a recipe for disaster. Remember, your partner may need you for your support of his or her nil. Opposite or "twin" nils are rarely successful (less than five percent).

9. A singleton or doubleton high trump, or a lengthy (4- or 5-card) trump suit is a strong deterrent to a nil bid. You cannot assume your partner has the key cards to relieve you.

10. The use of the blind nil bid should be reserved for desperate situations (only). Never start a game with this bid. You must be losing by at least 150 points (or more) to consider a blind nil option.

Chapter Seven

BIDDING QUIZ

Here are twenty hands (and a bonus hand) for you to test your bidding skills. Please review each holding carefully and then consider the optimum bid. What is your bid for each of these hands? (The answers are listed after the last question).

A   YOU BID FIRST: DETERMINE YOUR OPENING "SALVO", AND GIVE EACH HAND YOUR BEST "SHOT"!

1. ♠ – Q J 3   ♡ – A K 8   ◇ – 10 9 7 3   ♣ – A 9 2
2. ♠ – 10 9 8 6   ♡ – Q 4 3 2   ◇ – 5   ♣ – K 9 8 6
3. ♠ – A K Q J 9 8 ♡ – K Q J   ◇ – VOID   ♣ – K Q 9 2
4. ♠ – 6 5 2   ♡ – A Q 9 6 3 2 ◇ – 7 3   ♣ – 8 4
5. ♠ – K 10 9 8   ♡ – K 7 3   ◇ – K 4 2   ♣ – K 7 3

B   YOU BID IN SECOND POSITION — YOUR RIGHT HAND OPPONENT HAS OPENED WITH A THREE BID. WHAT IS YOUR BID (FOR EACH HAND)?

6. ♠ – A Q 3   ♡ – J 10 9 5 4   ◇ – A 9 4 2   ♣ – 7
7. ♠ – VOID   ♡ – Q J 10 3   ◇ – K J 9 8 6 ♣ – Q 10 9 7

C YOU ARE IN SECOND POSITION — YOUR RIGHT HAND
OPPONENT HAS OPENED WITH A NIL BID. NOW IT IS
YOUR TURN — WHAT IS YOUR BID FOR EACH HAND?

8 ♠ – Q J 10 2   ♡ – A Q 5   ◊ – K Q 6 4   ♣ – A K
9 ♠ – K 10 4   ♡ – J 7   ◊ – A 10 6 5 2 ♣ – J 6 2

D YOU BID IN THIRD POSITION — YOUR PARTNER OPENS
WITH A FOUR, THE RIGHT HAND OPPONENT BIDS TWO.
GO AHEAD — PLACE YOUR BID FOR EACH HAND.

10 ♠ – K Q 3   ♡ – A 4 2   ◊ – 7 6 4 2   ♣ – 10 8 5
11 ♠ – 7 5 3   ♡ – Q 7 6 3 2 ◊ – J 7 2   ♣ – 8 4

E YOU BID IN THIRD POSITION — YOUR PARTNER OPENS
WITH A NIL, THE RIGHT HAND OPPONENT BIDS SIX.
THINK CAREFULLY AND PLACE YOUR BID FOR EACH
HAND.

12 ♠ – K J 10   ♡ – K Q 9   ◊ – A K 2   ♣ – Q 10 8 3
13 ♠ – 10 6 2   ♡ – 10 9 8 3   ◊ – J 8 7 4   ♣ – Q 7
14 ♠ – A K J 9   ♡ – VOID   ◊ – K Q 9 6   ♣ – Q J 10 6 4
15 ♠ – K   ♡ – A K Q 7 5 2 ◊ – Q J 4 3   ♣ – K J

F YOU BID IN FOURTH POSITION — THE LEFT OPPONENT
OPENS WITH FOUR, PARTNER BIDS FIVE AND THE RIGHT
HAND OPPONENT BIDS NIL. YOU HAVE THE LAST BID FOR
EACH HAND. MAKE YOUR SELECTIONS.

16 ♠ – J 10 8 4 ♡ – K Q 9 2   ◊ - A K   ♣ – Q J 6
17 ♠ – VOID   ♡ – A K 8 7   ◊ – K Q 9 7 3 ♣ – A 8 6 5
18 ♠ – 7 3   ♡ – J 7 5 2   ◊ – A J 6 5 2 ♣ – J 3

G YOU BID IN FOURTH POSITION — THE LEFT HAND OPPO-
NENT OPENS WITH FIVE, PARTNER BIDS NIL AND THE

RIGHT HAND OPPONENT ALSO BIDS FIVE. ONCE AGAIN, YOU HAVE THE LAST BID FOR EACH HAND. GO FOR IT!

19 ♠ – 3 2	♡ – A 8 6 5 4 2	◊ – Q 7 4	♣ – Q 5
20 ♠ – A K 4 2	♡ – K 7 6	◊ – A Q 5	♣ – 10 9 5

BONUS QUESTION — THIS HAND ACTUALLY OCCURRED IN A TOURNAMENT. YOU HAVE THE OPENING BID. STEP UP TO THE PLATE AND TAKE A SWING AT THIS "CURVE BALL"!

21 ♠ – J 10 9 7 6 5 2 ♡ – VOID   ◊ – VOID   ♣ – Q J 10 8 6 3

ANSWERS TO BIDDING QUIZ

1. Bid FOUR — This is very clear cut, as you have three top tricks and a probable trump trick.

2. Bid ONE — A nil bid here is very suspect, especially with long middle spades and weak clubs.

3. Bid EIGHT — You have five sure trump tricks, two hearts and one club. With normal distribution, you could make an extra trick. A bid of nine is very greedy and not guaranteed. (Why throw away a sure 80 points in order to grab another 10 points?)

4. Bid NIL — The heart suit, despite its great length, is perfectly safe.

5. Bid FOUR — This is a brutal hand. It is reasonable to assume you will win two trumps and two of the side Kings. You may score three trumps if the Ace and another honor card appear on the same trick. If you have the opening lead, you will have to underlead one of the Kings. I would be inclined to bid three and hope that any extra tricks I took would be of help to my partner. An extra bag or two is acceptable in this situation. You may also be able to dump a winner if you have secured your bid.

6. Bid THREE — You should score two trumps (one via a club ruff or successful finesse) and the diamond Ace.

7. Bid ONE — A nil is out of the question with so many middle cards. This hand may get nailed for some baggage; however, can you really assume that the Queens will win tricks?

8. Bid SIX — You have an outside chance to score seven tricks. Why risk a sure 60 points.? Another factor is the possibility of sacrificing a later trick to take a shot at setting the nil.

9. Bid TWO — There just isn't any more horsepower in this hand.

10. Bid TWO — You hope to score two trumps and the Ace of hearts, but you can't assume the spades are favorably positioned or that your partner holds the Ace of trump.

11. Bid NIL — If your partner cannot help you in diamonds, then it is just not your day.

12. Bid FOUR — Normally a five bid would be in order, but you must consider that you will be covering your partner's nil. You may have to sacrifice a diamond trick. The loss of your bid is picayune to the loss of your partner's nil. A four bid should make rather easily with this hand.

13. Bid ONE — Don't even consider nil! Two opposite nils are a luscious target for the enemy to attack. Your club suit is very weak; your spade ten could be attacked, and you cannot expect any help from your partner.

14. Bid (a safe) THREE — Count on two trump tricks and a diamond, or three trumps. If you were not protecting a nil, then a four bid would be reasonable.

15. Bid TWO — You hope to take a heart trick and a black King, but remember your first obligation is to "COVER" your partner.

16. Bid THREE — Beware of duplication in your partner's suits. When both players on the same team are fighting for tricks in the same suits, there is trouble in "River City"! There is little hope of setting the nil, and thus, you must settle for eighty points. Note — you have a "fair" chance of pulling down the enemy four bid.

17. Bid THREE — This is just about as much as you can expect opposite your partner's five bid. There is a slightly better chance to attack the nil bid, but ensuring your eighty points is a higher priority.

18. Bid NIL — If your partner is unable to overtake your Jack of clubs, it is time to try another card game. How about a nice game of Cribbage?

19. Bid ONE — two opposite nils are a bad bet and there is no way that your partner can save you in either minor suit. You may even get set while helping your partner. Bid your one — if you are set, the loss of ten points to ensure a nil is a very good deal!

20. Bid THREE — You plan on sacrificing a trick or two in order to cover your partner.

21. (Bonus hand) — Bid FIVE — You have no way of predicting the number of trumps you will score, however a suit of this length should be worth at least four tricks. This is a very strange hand; a double void occurs approximately once every 12,000 deals. If your partner has as little as the Ace of clubs and the Ace of spades, you have a chance to make ten or even eleven tricks. However, if your partner has nothing of value in the black suits and high cards in the red suits, his or her hand is worthless to you. Your length in trumps will enable you to lead the suit and perhaps, "crash" some of the honor cards together (on the same tricks). These types of hands are very difficult to evaluate. In Bridge, the holder of a long major suit and a highly distributional hand usually makes a pre-emptive bid at the three level. However, I would be willing to say that the best Bridge players would be hard-pressed to "scientifically" reach an optimal contract with this hand. In the game of Spades, we have just one bid, and it is best to use a more controlled and conservative approach.

Chapter Eight

ILLUSTRATIVE HAND

The time has come to demonstrate a typical hand. In this book we will follow these basic guidelines.

A. The opening bid is made by the player to the immediate left of the dealer.

B. The opening lead is made by the player to the immediate right of the dealer.

Let us look at this rather interesting hand:

NORTH
♠ K 10 9
♡ J 9 7 4 3
♢ 6 4
♣ 8 7 4

WEST
♠ J 8 7 4 3 2
♡ VOID
♢ K 8 5 2
♣ A 5 2

EAST
♠ VOID
♡ Q 10 8 6 5
♢ A Q J 3
♣ J 9 6 3

SOUTH (Dealer)
♠ A Q 6 5
♡ A K 2
♢ 10 9 7
♣ K Q 10

45

BIDDING

NOTE: ASSUME THAT THE LOWEST CARD IS PLAYED IF A
SPECIFIC CARD IS NOT INDICATED.

WEST	NORTH	EAST	SOUTH
5	2	1	5

A quick review of the bidding is in order. West expected to take at
least three trump tricks with a reasonable chance for a fourth trump as
well. A sure bet was the Ace of clubs. There was also a good chance to
score the King of diamonds. North expected two trump tricks,
although this might have been a bit ambitious. East counted on the Ace
of diamonds and might have been tempted to bid two; however, his
partner's bid restrained him. South's bid of five was quite reasonable
with three top tricks and the likely possibility of an additional trick in
each black suit. If anything, his bid was on the conservative side, but he
felt that seven was a very good contract. The combined bid of 13 tricks
for both sides created an air of tension as the possibility of a set was
quite high.

East was reluctant to open with a diamond and chose a safe club
lead — the three. South inserted the ten — a somewhat risky play
here — and West flew with the Ace. The club five went to South's King
as North played the eight and East played the nine. The King of hearts
was trotted out and South expressed shock at the appearance of
West's deuce of spades. Another club by West was taken by South's
Queen and the diamond ten was placed on the table. West played low
and East was thrilled to win the free finesse with his Queen. East now
grabbed the Ace of diamonds as his partner concealed a wry grin. It is
usually a good idea to take an extra trick or two to help relieve pressure
on your partner as long as you don't accumulate bags. Note — bags are
not applicable here, as the trick total is thirteen. East finally led the Jack
of diamonds as West played low and North ruffed with the spade ten.
A low heart was covered by the six and the Ace and another small
trump by West. West now led his diamond King, yielding a ruff-sluff.
North discarded a heart as South trumped with his spade six. South
now chose the spade five lead at this junction. West inserted the four
and North finessed his nine (rather than rise with the King).

North next led the heart nine which fetched the ten and deuce of hearts and the spade eight from West. Finally West had to lead into South's Ace-Queen combination and the hand was claimed for the last two tricks. It's too bad that the Ace, King and Queen of spades clashed together on the final-two tricks, but that's the way the cards fell. This was a hard fought hand by both sides, as both teams scrambled home with their contracts. This is a good example of cooperative partnership play.

ILLUSTRATIVE HAND

ORDER OF TRICKS TAKEN

TRICK #	EAST	SOUTH	WEST	NORTH
1	♣ — 3	♣ — 10	♣ — A *	♣ — 4
2	♣ — 9	♣ — K *	♣ — 5	♣ — 8
3	♡ — 5	♡ — K	♠ — 2 *	♡ — 3
4	♣ — 6	♣ — Q *	♣ — 2	♣ — 7
5	◊ — Q *	◊ — 10	◊ — 2	◊ — 4
6	◊ — A *	◊ — 7	◊ — 5	◊ — 6
7	◊ — J	◊ — 9	◊ — 8	♠ — 10 *
8	♡ — 6	♡ — A	♠ — 3 *	♡ — 4
9	◊ — 3	♠ — 6 *	◊ — K	♡ — 7
10	♣ — J	♠ — 5	♠ — 4	♠ — 9 *
11	♡ — 10	♡ — 2	♠ — 8 *	♡ — 9
12	♡ — 8	♠ — A *	♠ — 7	♠ — K
13	♡ — Q	♠ —Q *	♠ — J	♡ — J

*DENOTES TRICK TAKEN

SUMMARY   (2)   (5)   (4)   (2)

TOTAL – 13 TRICKS   North/South – 7 tricks   East/West – 6 tricks

Chapter Nine

PLAY OF THE HAND

After the bidding is completed, the opening lead is made and the hand begins. A complete review of leads will be made in a later chapter. The person to the right of the dealer commences play with a selection of the card which he deems to be the best possible choice. This can be a very critical decision, and the success of a contract is often hinged on the strength of an opening lead. Your objectives and order of priority in every hand are as follows:

A. The fulfillment of your bid (making your contract).

B. The support of your partner's bid, should that become necessary. This is especially true when your partner bids nil.

C. Setting the opponent's contract (if possible) with minimal risk to yours.

D. Avoiding capturing excessive bags. Watch those bags — they will kill you!

STANDARD NUMERICAL (NON-NIL) BIDS:

Assuming you have reached the optimal contract (which is difficult to ascertain early in the hand), your immediate priority is **making your bid**. The bidding usually provides a reasonable amount of information, and will help you to develop "a game plan." If you have a good partner, he/she will take care of business from that side of the table. When you are on lead, a very logical choice is a solid suit headed by a sequence (e.g., A K Q, K Q J, Q J 10, etc.) A lead of a singleton "spot" card is also effective. However, if you are defending against an opponent's nil, **your strategy needs to be adjusted**. (Refer to chapter eleven.) Here, we will review the play of standard (number) contracts. Try to avoid underleading Aces or Kings, as you may hand unexpected tricks to your opponents. This is fine if you are trying to escape bags towards the end of a hand; however, you must ensure fulfilling your contract **first**. A very good technique is the clearing of singletons or doubletons from your hand in order to pave the way for **ruffing**. The play of spades is usually delayed until the later stages of the hand. Sometimes the opponents will do the work for you and lead advantageously into your hand or allow you to make key discards.

If you have secured your bid, it is important to keep an eye on your partner's progress. It may be necessary to help your partner — even if you have to take an extra trick or two. It is considered good strategy to lead with your partner's short suit which will enable him to trump early. Of course, setting the opponent (after guaranteeing your contract) is ideal. The higher the combined bid for both teams, the more attractive a set becomes. We will explore this further in the chapter referencing defense. Just for the record, it does not pay to grab a fistful of bags in order to set middle and low level bids. If you have a chance to discard losers in order to avoid bags, it is best to unload unprotected middle cards. Another fine tactic is to reduce or shorten the length of a suit by making strategic discards on the suit in play. There are many situations where this is a much better choice than the use of a trump. It could allow you to score a needed ruff. Finally, if your right hand opponent leads with a low card, a good rule of thumb is to play a low card as well (referred to as a **second hand low**). There are a few exceptions and those are based on specific situations. This allows your partner a chance to win the trick. Don't grab Aces too quickly! Give your partner a chance to win a King or Queen in the fourth position. Nothing is more frustrating than to "fly" with an Ace prematurely and swallow up your partner's King or Queen. Another trusty rule of thumb is the **third hand high**. If two small cards are played preceding your turn (in which case you are in "third position"), you should play your highest card unless you are trying to avoid a bag. Otherwise, the last player will win a trick cheaply with a low or middle card.

Sometimes, you will find yourself in a bit of trouble during the play of a hand. It is better to take an extra trick (which you were probably going to win anyway), and allow your partner an additional option. Observe very closely the cards which your partner leads and discards. If he or she is dumping high cards, it is probably a bag-avoidance maneuver. It is generally considered very bad technique to take a trick away from your partner unless you have a very good reason for doing so (e.g., returning a suit for partner to ruff). In most contracts, you must determine your sure winners first, and then try to develop tricks in those suits which are missing key honor cards. I cannot overemphasize the importance of controlling bags. It is useless to make contracts with overtricks on a regular basis. If this is occurring frequently, you and your partner need to have a discussion regarding your bidding styles.

NILS (COVERING)

Protecting your partner's nil bid is a key element of the game. This is referred to as **"covering a nil."** A nil bid is not ironclad. As a matter of fact, most nils have a weakness which I jokingly refer to as the "underbelly". Basically, it is a race between you and the defense. It does remind me a bit of the battles which occur in the game of bridge when no-trump contracts are in play! You are trying to protect potential weaknesses in your partner's hand and the defense is trying to force your partner to win a trick. The point value of a nil is just too great to ignore. This example will give you an understanding of just what is at stake. Suppose the score in a close game is tied — you and your opponents have 300 points each — your partner has bid nil, you have bid five, the opponents have bid six. If you fulfill your nil as well as your bid, you will reach 450 points. If your partner's nil is set and you make your bid, you will be at 250 points. An absolute disaster is to lose the nil and your bid, leaving you at 150 points. Thus, you can see the "swing" value of points for a nil is really 200 — the difference between making the nil and going set. You must go all out to protect or cover your partner — even at the cost of losing your bid. There is only one exception, and that is the setting of the opponent's **high level bid** and fulfillment of your own contract. For example: if the opponents have bid 10 or 11 tricks, your partner has bid nil, and you have the opportunity to set the opponents' contract, by all means go for it! The result will be a deduction of 100 or 110 points from your opponents' score — even if you partner loses his nil. Although this is a "wash" (trade-off) or sorts, it is important to deprive the "enemy" of such large gains. Basically, it depends once again, on the score at the time — especially if the opponents are approaching game. Often, you will see the opponents conceding your nil if the difference is advantageous to them.

When you are playing opposite your partner's nil, you should try to get the lead; however, if an opponent plays a high card, the best strategy is to allow that card to win. If you hold the K 9 8 of clubs and an opponent plays the Queen of clubs, grabbing the King could be an error since you may need to sacrifice it in order to protect your partner. If the Ace does not appear after two rounds of clubs you may deduce that your partner holds it and wants you to shift suits. A solid side suit of your own may allow your partner to make discards. For example: if you hold A Q 9 8 5 of diamonds, your best play is to lead with the Ace. Should your partner hold the King, he will drop it under the Ace and you can continue with the Queen. This will allow your partner to get rid of another middle diamond. Hopefully, he will not hold the K J 10 of this suit without a low card, otherwise you may question his nil bid. Your partner, having a void in a suit, presents an ideal situation for support. Simply lead with any card — preferably the highest one in your partner's void suit — which will enable him to make more discards of dangerous cards, especially Aces. If trumps have been "broken", then lead your highest spades. You must assume that your partner did not bid nil with a natural trump trick. Some experienced players prefer to save a trump or two — in the event it becomes necessary to ruff a possible losing card in a partner's weak side suit. And now for some "no-nos" regarding the protection of a nil bid:

A. **Never lead a low card!** It is the kiss of death for a nil and your partner will not be a happy camper. The lead of a low card will probably be followed by a low card by your left hand opponent, and your
partner may be forced to win a chintzy middle card trick.

B. **Do not lead middle cards of a suit if you have higher cards in the
same suit.** This may force an honor card from your partner's hand.

C. **Do not overtake a high card played by an opponent.** For example:
If you hold the Ace of clubs, and the opponent leads the King or
Queen, save your Ace for later. Your partner may need it to discard
a middle club.

D. **Never lead a middle or low trump** (especially if you hold the Ace
or King). Your partner may get "skewered" with a ten, Jack or
Queen.

E. Do not overruff the opponents' play of a spade on a side suit. Save
your middle or high spades (for the end of the hand).

PLAYING A NIL

If you have a steady, dependable partner, half of your battle is over.
Nothing instills more confidence than knowing that when the going
gets tough, your partner is there for you. Assess your hand for any
potential weaknesses. Sometimes you may need to take a chance and
play a middle or high card early, hoping for help from your partner. For
example: if you have a balanced hand and you hold the ten and two of
hearts, your best play is the ten of hearts, even if this is an opening lead.
Unless your partner has bid one or two, it is very reasonable to assume
that he has at least the Jack of hearts. The odds of the opponents holding all four heart honors are less than five percent. However, if you are
void in a suit, or hold a singleton, you may try to obtain a heart discard.
Lead your singleton or a safe side suit and try to give the lead to your partner for a favorable return. If possible, save critical low cards of the same
suit for the end of a hand. Remember, long suits with lots of low cards are
usually safe. There is no need to discard any cards from these suits. Instead
try to discard dangerous middle or high cards of other suits. If trumps
have been broken, underruffing a trump trick is generally a good idea, as

long as your remaining trump or trumps are not vulnerable. Finally, counting suits and remembering spot cards is a real plus. There are just too many players who "fly by the seat of their pants" or play by "instinct." If you place too much reliance on random luck, then sooner or later you will be burned. When playing nils, make the effort to track honor cards and the number of cards played in your critical suits. Nothing is more frustrating than to make the wrong discard at the end of the hand and be forced to win the last trick with a card you could have unloaded earlier. It's worth it to make the effort and earn the reward.

PLAY OF THE HAND — REVIEW

Here are some hands for play — plan analysis.

Note — "LHO" denotes left hand opponent; "Pard" denotes Partner; "RHO" denotes right hand opponent.

HAND 1. Your LHO bids two; Pard bids four; RHO bids two; and you bid four. The opening lead is the Jack of diamonds from your RHO. You hold:

♠ — K 10 5   ♡ — A K 4   ◇ — Q 3 2   ♣ — A J 10 2

Cover with the Queen of diamonds, as you want to shed this card early. (It may also help to promote the King for Pard). If your LHO wins this trick, you will be in good shape if he shifts to a club. This will allow for later options depending on which club appears on the first round. When you get the lead, play the Ace of hearts, followed by the King. If both of these win, then continue with the heart four. You should be able to score a trump trick, as well as the Ace of clubs, making four. If a high heart is ruffed on the second round, you need to try for two spade tricks or two club tricks. Perhaps your partner will be able to help you here. The opponents will be "gunning" for you, as you have an eight bid on the table, and they can take a few bags in exchange for a set. If the Ace of hearts is ruffed on the first round, then call in the "dogs" and give up the hunt.

NOTE: FOR INSTRUCTIONAL PURPOSES, SOME OF THE OPEN-
ING BID AND LEAD POSITIONS HAVE BEEN ADJUSTED IN THE
ILLUSTRATED EXAMPLES.

HAND 2. Pard opens the round of bidding with a nil; RHO bids
five; you bid three (your normal bid would be four), and the LHO bids
three. The lead is Queen of hearts from LHO. Your partner plays the
nine. You hold:

♠ — J 10 2   ♡ — A 10 6   ◊ — A Q 4   ♣ — K Q 8 7

Assuming that your RHO plays low, duck the Queen of hearts with
the six. Save your Ace of hearts for later protection. Your partner may
have another middle dangerous heart. If LHO now shifts to a club,
duck this as well, unless your partner is winning the trick with a middle card. When a heart is led, step up with the Ace and cash the ten of
hearts. (If Pard held the heart Jack, it would have been discarded on the
Queen, and if he held the heart King, that would have gone under the
Ace. Thus the ten is clean! Resist the lure of the diamond suit, and play
the King of clubs. A lot of scenarios are dependent on leads by defend-
ers. Finally, if your partner produces the Ace of clubs or a spade honor
(and either wins a trick), pretend that you have an upset stomach and
ask to be excused from the table.

HAND 3. You bid five, LHO bids four, Pard bids one and RHO bids
two. The opening lead is the four of diamonds by your RHO. You hold:

♠ — A K 8 4   ♡ — K 7 2   ◊ — A K 2   ♣ — Q J 3

You have four top tricks in spades and diamonds. In order to fulfill
your ambitious bid of five, you must hope to win the King of hearts, a
club honor or a long trump. I would have bid four with this hand; however, we are in five and that's the way it is. Take the Ace-King of diamonds, followed by the two; maybe your partner will be able to ruff the
third round. If a heart is now led and the Ace appears, you have your
fifth trick. If the Ace does not appear, then you must play the King and
hope that the Ace is in a favorable position. If the heart suit does not

behave for you, then you are reduced to desperation and must hope that you can score a club honor. The opponents are clearly marked with the high spades, and the Queen-Jack of trump are probably positioned in back of your Ace-King and two spot cards. Then again, your partner may realize your plight and perhaps take an extra trick for you.

HAND 4. Pard bids three; RHO bids three; you bid four; and your LHO bids three.

♠ — K 9 5 3   ♡ — 4   ◊ — K Q 6 4   ♣ — A 5 3 2

This is a "pattern" hand. Once again, your bid is somewhat aggressive but considering the distribution it is reasonable. One thing is for sure — the total number of tricks is thirteen, and both sides need to be on their toes. You hope to use your low spades for ruffs in the heart suit.

The opening lead is the Queen of clubs from the LHO. Pard plays low (probably denying the King), and you hop up with the Ace. Now, you play your low heart. Surely, he has an honor card in hearts or an entry in diamonds which will provide the impetus for a heart return. **As in Bridge or Whist, it is usually a good idea to return your partner's first led suit. However, consider the overall situation before making this "automatic" play.**

The plan is to ruff two hearts and win a guaranteed four tricks. The alternative is to ruff one heart and take the spade King later. You are already assured of a trick in each minor suit barring unusual distribution. If your Pard has a solid three bid, you have a good chance of setting the opponents as well.

HAND 5. Pard bids four: RHO opponent bids three; you bid six, and LHO bids a very predictable nil. The opening lead from your right hand opponent is the Ace of diamonds. You hold:

♠ — A K 10 9 8 3 ♡ — K Q J 10 4 ◊ — Void   ♣ — A 7

Your bid is quite reasonable especially considering the strength of your spade suit. Once again, thirteen tricks are on the table. This seemingly simple hand is quite complicated, and full of multiple variations.

A lot of the hands in the *Advanced Play and Strategy* are of this genre. Setting the nil is a very remote possibility — you must try to make your bid, and hold the loss of points to 30 (for the hand). Another plan now hatches. The nil bidder is on your left, and will not be able to attack your bid (or take defensive tricks). Nailing his partner's three bid will give you a small profit for the hand. Ruff the diamond lead with the spade three, and immediately lead with the spade ten. (An alternative choice is to discard the seven of clubs on the first trick which allows for later ruffing possibilities in the club suit.) Your lead of the ten of spades may let your partner score the Queen or play the Jack and force the Queen out. It's okay if your partner has only two spot cards in trump — as long as the LHO followed to the first round. The ten loses to a spade honor on the right, and you are still in good shape. Your partner will be able to lead a spade for a finesse through the other spade honor (on the right). If a high diamond is returned at this point, ruff it low and force out the heart Ace. A club lead is stronger — rather than allow us to score all of our trump individually. We take the club Ace, and shift to the heart TEN. This will make Pard play the Ace if he has it. Now a spade return by Pard is deadly. But the worst case scenario now happens. Let's assume that our RHO holds the heart Ace. My goodness, what did your partner have for his four bid? Our very capable RHO now continues with the King of diamonds — the best defense. We ruff with the nine of trump. Now, we play the Ace-King of Spades. If distributions are normal, the remaining honor will fall. Once again the worst happens. The Queen of spades does not drop, as our RHO held four spades. We ignore the Master Trump which is outstanding in the enemy hand and proceed to cash out the heart suit. The RHO can take his spade Queen whenever he likes, and we limit the loss to two trump and the heart Ace. (I know — some of you may ask, "How about the King of clubs?") Well, I suppose that our friendly RHO could have THIS card as well. In that case, the whole hand was hopelessly "stacked," and Pard should have bid nil as well! The play of the hand in spades is very comparable to the play of the hand in bridge. An expert player at the helm will bring in many contracts and work cooperatively with his or her partner to set the opponents' bids. Practice is the best way to "hone" your skills.

Chapter Ten

THE FINESSE

A finesse is an attempt to win a trick with a lesser card. Suppose you need two tricks to fulfill your contract or to set the opponents. You are coming down to the end of a hand. You hold the Ace and Queen of hearts. Your partner, who has already made his bid, leads the eight of hearts, your right hand opponent plays the nine in normal cadence (We will come to the topic of hesitations later in this section.) What do you do? If you take your Ace, you will lose the Queen to the King no matter which opponent holds the monarch. Your partner probably does not hold the King as he already has made his bid and would not under lead that card. Another indication is his lead of a heart, which is probably a neutral suit. Your best chance (50 percent) is to play the Queen. If the left hand opponent has the King you would have lost it anyway. However, if your right hand opponent has the King, the Queen will win the trick, and you will now score your Ace on the next round of hearts. Although 50 percent is not a guarantee, it is far better than zero percent. Should you hold the same Ace–Queen combination in spades, winning two tricks with a successful finesse is guaranteed.

Finesses come in all types and shapes. There is the common A-Q specimen, as well as a the rare "ruffing" variety (K-Q-J opposite a void). Here is another example. Suppose you hold K x or K x x of a suit. Your partner has already made her bid, you are in need of one more trick to make yours. A lead from your left and opponent is ideal — as you will get to play the King in fourth position or duck if the Ace shows up. If your partner or right hand opponent leds this suit, and the Ace does not appear, you must play the King. If you play small, your left hand opponent may win the trick with the Queen; thus, your best chance is to play the King. Why? Well, if your left hand opponent has the Ace, your King is dead anyway. If your partner has the Ace, your King is the winner (it is unlikely that your partner holds the Ace in this situation as she has already made her bid). The key is your right hand opponent — and if he holds the Ace, your King wins. If your right hand opponent leads a small card of this suit, an exception to the "second hand low" adage applies. At this point, you must play the King and hope that your left hand opponent does not hold the Ace. There are also situations in a close contract where the play of the King will promote the Queen for your partner if he or she happens to hold her. If the Ace and Queen are on your left, your King would be dead anyway unless your left hand opponent grabbed the Ace earlier in the hand. We cannot always expect our opponents to do our work for us. There are instances where we will win ("free" finesses) and these usually occur when the left hand opponent underleads his honor cards and allows you to score a King or A-Q combination. There is an impulse to grab your top tricks and sometimes this is correct especially when avoiding bags. However, there are many situations where you will need to manufacture a trick, and a finesse is a convenient way to accomplish this. Here is a table of finessing scenarios and the proper card to play. Assume that a small card has been led and it is your turn to play.

*** FINESSING GUIDELINE CHART ***

# of Tricks Needed	You Hold These Cards	Lead From Right Hand Opponent or Partner	Proper Play (Specific Card)	Comment
2	A Q x	X	Q	Use only if you need two tricks or are trying to set the opponents
2	A Q xx	X	Q	Slightly higher risk with longer holdings
2	A Q xxx	X	A	With a long suit, take the Ace and forget the finesse
1	K x	X	K	Your only chance
1	K xx	X	K	Your only chance
1	K xxx (x)	X	K	It's now or never!
2	A Q 10	X	Q	Correct, if only two tricks are needed
3	A Q 10 x	X	10	Your only hope is that K J are on the right — called "double" finesse
2	K Q x (x)	X	K	Your best chance
1	K J xx (x)	X	K	Similar to above example
2	K J x (x)	X	J	You must hope A Q are on right
3	A K J (x)	X	J	Desperate situation
2	A K J (x)	X	A	Forget about three tricks!
2	A J 10 (x)	X	J	Standard technique / "repeating" finesse

1. Assume RHO plays a low card prior to your play.
2. If your LHO was on lead you would have no problem at all!

SUMMARY OF FINESSES

Review the finessing guide table above and commit to memory the basic combinations listed. Please note that in some instances you may have to surrender the lead in order to repeat the finesse in the same suit at a later interval. The purpose of the finesse is to try to establish and promote tricks with lesser cards and it may provide salvation in an otherwise lost situation. It is also essential to consider when to finesse and when not to finesse. Long suits reduce the potential for successful finesses. It is particularly aggravating to take a losing finesse, e.g., with an A-Q combination and then have your Ace trumped on the next round leaving you with nothing. The objective is to insure your contract without becoming "finesse-happy." Another important consideration is the accumulation of bags. Therefore, use the finesse wisely but do not become overly dependent on it. The wreckage of many "overfinessed" hands is littered on the reefs and shoals of the "Island of Spades."

Chapter Eleven

DEFENSIVE PLAY AND TECHNIQUE

Defense is one of the essential elements of the game of spades. While it is imperative to fulfill your contracts, it is equally compelling to defend the opponents' bids properly. Many a game is lost by poor or improper technique which allows impossible nils or borderline contracts to be successfully made. Your primary directive is to make your bid with minimal bagging. However, if you are in danger of defeat (set) or you have already been set, you must switch your attention to defense. The time has come to attack your opponents' contract. Of course, the best of everything is the completion of your bid and defeat of the opponents' bid at the same time. It does happen occasionally and produces a wonderful feeling of accomplishment.

As mentioned previously, the greatest opportunity to set the opponents is when the **total of all tricks bid equals 12 or 13**. This allows for the minimal accumulation of bags. After you ensure your contract, you can go for the set with complete confidence. If the total number of tricks exceeds 13 (this also happens occasionally with aggressive bidding) it provides an "every man for himself" scenario. In this case, once you make your bid, the opponents now are set. To be an outstanding defender, you must also be an aggressive player. The old adage, "the best defense is a good offense" certainly does apply. In Spades, there is no dummy hand, and no specific suit or "no-trump" bids. Thus, you must interpret information by analyzing the opponents' plays, signals, and discards. **Your partner is the most important part of your defensive effort.** If you just sit there and ignore the meanings of his plays and discards, you'll greatly diminish your chance of a successful defense. The road to a successful defense begins with the **opening lead.**

The game of Spades is relatively new compared to Bridge. Plenty of books have been written about Bidding systems, and play of the hand. While some of these do have a true relevance to Spades, most are merely useful guidelines. Defense is a different proposition, and its strategy is universal.

OPENING LEADS

When the round of bidding is over, the player on the right hand side of the dealer makes the opening lead. He must think in a dual fashion — how can I ensure my team's contract, and how can I set the opponents' contract? The best players in the world do not always make the best lead — but they are savvy enough to be familiar with the combinations and percentages which produce results. Opening leads are not exercises in clairvoyance or serendipity. There are logical and straightforward techniques. Lastly, we must consider leads against nil bids, as well as leads against numerical (non-nil) contracts. Incidentally, if you are on lead against **your partner's nil bid,** this is part of "covering" or protecting his nil. We discussed this in an earlier section.

Here some useful and general "tips" for leads against "standard" or numerical contracts. If you have a **singleton** in a side suit, lead it. The only exception to this is the lead of a singleton King which may give a free trick to the offense.

A. Lead the top card from any doubleton such as the nine– three, or Ace–six. This applies to spot card doubletons or Ace doubletons only. Leading with a spot card, and then playing a lower spot card of the same suit in the next round alerts your partner that you are now void in that suit. In Bridge, this is called a "high-low" or "echo" signal.

B. Lead the King from any sequence combination including King-Queen or Ace-King. **Refer to opening lead table at end of this chapter.**

C. Do not underlead Aces, Kings or Queens.

D. It is acceptable to lead a weak neutral suit consisting of spot cards if you do not have a comfortable alternative; e.g., if you hold 9 8 7 of a suit, lead the 7. If you then play the 8 on the next round, your partner will know that you started with at least three cards in that suit.

DEFENSE AGAINST NIL BIDS

Defending the enemy's nil bid can be a very daunting task. Some players are absolutely intimidated when they hear the word "nil" from either opponent. If all nils were sound, then we would not waste our time defending them. As I said before, most nils have an "underbelly" that can be exposed with proper defense. Remember, you are working with a partner and good communication is vital.

A nil is a trick-avoidance bid; therefore, the defense should also think in reverse. The partner of the nil-bidder will be doing everything he can to ensure the success of the nil — and this includes sacrificing his own bid, if necessary. A lot of "botched" nils are due to poor coop-eration between the nil-bidder and his partner. Your job is to confuse the nil bidder or his partner and induce an erroneous play. Here are some useful tips for "breaking" the opponents' nils: Remember, it is important to make your high level bids (seven or more), and the score will dictate your options. Low bids at the one to four level can and should be sacrificed if the nil can be attacked efficiently.

"NIL-BUSTING" (TEN "EASY" STEPS)!

1. If you have the opening lead, and you hold a long **sequence of low cards** in the **same** suit, begin your attack here. This will force the nil

bidder's partner to use his "covering" cards in the same suit pre-maturely. An alternative is the lead of middle cards, but this is much less effective.

2. A very strong defense is the lead of a **singleton or doubleton** — espe-cially if it is a spot card. This will prepare for the **breaking of trump** — a very vital part of the defense. In addition, you (the defender) will now be able to discard other useless high (or mid-dle) cards. (You might even get "lucky" and catch a stranded high card in the nil bidder's hand.)

3. Do not lead or cash high cards in suits that are **lengthy**. This will allow the nil bidder to discard losers, and will accumulate bags for you, as well.

4. If your partner leads a low card, and the nil bidder's partner also plays low (for any reason), then it is vital to play your lowest card as well. The nil bidder may be forced to win this trick.

5. If you hold one or two (**and no more**) middle or high cards in a suit, and do not have a natural low-card lead, by all means, get these "puppies" out of the way. Please note that this must be done very **early** in the hand before either opponent has a chance to dis-card in this suit. Although some "strategists" will argue against this technique, I am prepared to defend this maneuver. I cannot see the value of leaving a high singleton or doubleton combination of cards in your hand, while shifting to another suit.

6. The most effective defense against a nil is the **"breaking" and con-trolled subsequent lead of spades**. The idea is to **remove the trump from the partner of the nil bidder** and prevent possible ruffs in weak suits. This can be a very delicate maneuver, as you do not want to allow a critical discard on excessive spade leads. Leads of middle and then low spades are quite good, and may flush out an exposed spade-honor or weak-middle card, such as the nine or ten from the nil bidder's hand. There is always a risk in "flushing trump"; however, experience has shown that breaking it is a good strategy against nils. An alternative strategy used by many experts is the use of high spades for ruffing. The idea is to promote a middle

spade in the nil-bidder's hand. This technique will be reviewed in *Win at Spades: Advanced Play and Strategy*.

7. Do not lead a suit in which the nil bidder is void. This is a horrible play, and allows for easy discards.

8. Another equally putrid play is the yielding of a **"ruff-sluff."** This occurs after the lead of any suit in which both of the opponents are void, and usually occurs toward the middle or end of the hand. (The nil bidder makes a discard while his partner trumps or the nil bidder underruffs his partner's higher trump.)

9. If your side has a contract of **eight or more tricks** on the table, **your strategy should shift.** The first priority is the success of your bid. If the nil appears to be impregnable, his "partner" may be vulnerable. He will be conceding tricks early in the hand, which may weaken his own bid, Most importantly, he cannot expect any support from a nil-bidding partner — who is in no position to offer any help! Should his bid be in the range of three — five tricks (with an eight or nine trick contract by your side), by all means, go for the **set of the nil bidder's partner.** As we said previously, when the combined total of tricks equals 12 or 13, it is worthwhile going for the set. This is one of the very few instances in which an enemy's nil bid is ignored. Another instance occurs when the nil bid is inconsequential; your side will win the game or amass a huge lead — even if the nil makes.

10. The key for success is the **attention to detail** — observing your partner's suit, counting signals, attacking trump early, avoiding poor leads, and probing for the weak suit. It really is worthwhile to establish a reputation as a "Nil Buster"! This will have a psychological effect on the opponents, and may even deter them from more nil bidding.

STANDARD OPENING LEAD SUMMARY
(AGAINST STANDARD-NUMERICAL BID-CONTRACTS)

CARDS HELD	SUGGESTED LEAD
A K Q (x)	King
A K Q J	King
A K J(x)	King
A K xxx	King
A Q x(x)	Do not lead from this holding
K Q J	King
K Q x(x)	King
Kxx(x)	Do not lead from this holding
Q J 10(x)	Queen
Q Jx(x)	Do not lead from this holding
J 10 9x	Jack

Please note that these leads do not apply against nil bids. If your partner has bid nil, the lead of a very long and strong suit is ideal. If either opponent has bid nil, your best lead is a middle or low card. (Refer to review of "nil" defense).

Chapter Twelve

ILLUSTRATIVE HANDS

HAND # 1 — "FREE FINESSES"

NORTH
♠ Q 10 5
♡ J 9 6
◊ 8 6 5 4 2
♣ J 4

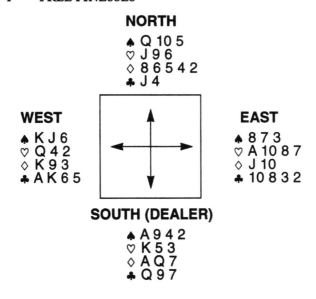

WEST
♠ K J 6
♡ Q 4 2
◊ K 9 3
♣ A K 6 5

EAST
♠ 8 7 3
♡ A 10 8 7
◊ J 10
♣ 10 8 3 2

SOUTH (DEALER)
♠ A 9 4 2
♡ K 5 3
◊ A Q 7
♣ Q 9 7

BIDDING

NOTE: ASSUME SMALLEST CARD IS PLAYED IF A CARD IS NOT SPECIFIED. THIS APPLIES TO ALL REMAINING HANDS.

WEST	NORTH	EAST	SOUTH
4	1	1	5

North/South needed 60 points to close out a game; thus South pushed for an extra trick in his bid. Bags were not of any significance, as each side had three. East led the deuce of clubs, South played the nine and West took the King, while North dropped the Jack. West continued with the Ace of clubs, as North completed his "high low" signal with the four, and East dumped the three and South played the seven. Now West shifted to the nine of diamonds — an absolutely abysmal defensive play! It was followed by North's eight, East's Jack, and South's Queen. South was pleased with the diamond gift and cashed his diamond Ace drawing three smaller cards. Now South tried the Queen of clubs which drew two small clubs and a diamond from North. Then South cleared the diamond suit with the lead of the seven as West played the King, North a small spot, and East trumped in with the eight of spades. This was another curious play! East grabbed the Ace of hearts which drew three small cards from the other players. His comment was, "That extra trick should help your partner." The spade seven was now led, with South playing the four, as West finessed his Jack. This lost to the Queen, and North promptly played the Jack of hearts. South took the King and cashed the Ace of spades as West played small. South's nine of spades now went to West's King and the rest of the hand was routine. Both sides made their contract and South was rewarded for his aggressive bidding. However, the East/West defense was the less than acceptable, as South barely broke a sweat. The guesses in the red suits were eliminated.

HAND 2 — 'GIVE ME A BREAK'

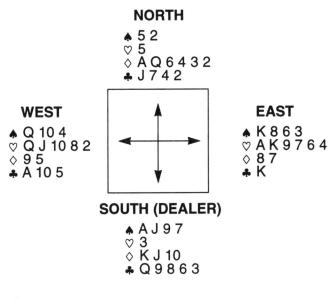

NORTH
♠ 5 2
♡ 5
◊ A Q 6 4 3 2
♣ J 7 4 2

WEST
♠ Q 10 4
♡ Q J 10 8 2
◊ 9 5
♣ A 10 5

EAST
♠ K 8 6 3
♡ A K 9 7 6 4
◊ 8 7
♣ K

SOUTH (DEALER)
♠ A J 9 7
♡ 3
◊ K J 10
♣ Q 9 8 6 3

BIDDING

WEST	NORTH	EAST	SOUTH
3	NIL	3	4

The score in the game was North/South 480 East/West 450. Bags were irrelevant as each side had three. When the round of bidding was completed North was pleased with his partner's four bid, and made the comment "it has been one heck of a game everybody." This was a subtle form of "table talk" indicating to his partner that he felt quite confident about his nil. It is really hard to fault North's nil bid. After all, it looked like a lead pipe cinch. East pondered his opening lead and started with the King of clubs. When the King held, East decided to probe the heart suit with the four. It was to be the "lead of the year"! Although South did not like his singleton, he felt that West probably had a middle or high heart or North had the deuce. However, West, who loved seeing the three from South, and in a display of serendipity, ducked with HIS deuce. The result was quite pleasing (and I am sure very appealing) when the five won the trick! North was absolutely shocked (an understatement) and immediately hurled several insults at his partner. Some of the comments included: "In case you forgot, partner, that was a nil I bid" and "I can't believe that the best heart you had was the three." This was followed by — "Why don't we just give them the game?" Finally a few choice profanities were uttered and the game abruptly ended.

Yes, it was quite incredible that North and South both held singleton low hearts and North's five was a winner. South with a nice collection of high cards in the other three suits was utterly unable to protect his partner. Certainly, this is an extreme example of duplication. Even though North later realized the unfortunate layout of the cards, his anger did not subside. He even went as far as suggesting that South trump the first round of hearts when the possibility of North taking the trick was apparent! (A revoke was a novel suggestion to be sure.) However, South had to follow suit and that was his crime. It suffices to say, that was the end of their partnership. The probabilities of two opposite singletons in the same suit occurring simultaneously are several hundred to one. When you consider that both singletons were very low cards, it made this deal almost unique.

HAND 3 — "BAG CITY"

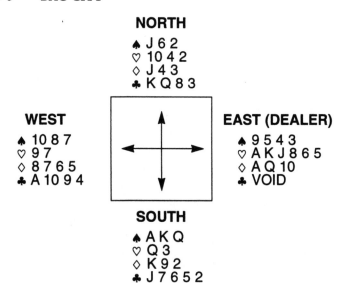

```
                    NORTH
                    ♠ J 6 2
                    ♥ 10 4 2
                    ◇ J 4 3
                    ♣ K Q 8 3

   WEST                              EAST (DEALER)
   ♠ 10 8 7                          ♠ 9 5 4 3
   ♥ 9 7                             ♥ A K J 8 6 5
   ◇ 8 7 6 5                         ◇ A Q 10
   ♣ A 10 9 4                        ♣ VOID

                    SOUTH
                    ♠ A K Q
                    ♥ Q 3
                    ◇ K 9 2
                    ♣ J 7 6 5 2
```

BIDDING

SOUTH	WEST	NORTH	EAST
3	1	1	2

The scores were close as East/West led North/South 470 to 430. It is also noteworthy that both sides had six bags each. East decided to bid conservatively upon hearing his partner's one bid as he felt that all they needed was three tricks to end the game. It was a very scientific analysis. What then followed was a lengthy dissertation by East regarding the mathematics and psychology of the game of spades. He commented that he was an expert and prided himself on technique. Finally, he said to South "This has been a great game, and you should not be ashamed of losing to us!" North led the King of clubs and East immediately pounced on this with the nine of spades. Now everyone was treated to a discussion about the merits of reducing trump length in order to save bags, and how the use of the nine was such a "sweet" play. The players now heard this utterance: "I'd better make sure of our bid," and he promptly cashed the Ace-King of hearts (leaving North with the deuce) as he played the ten and four. Next came the Ace of diamonds and assurance to his partner that an extra bag or two would be "peanuts." East's final comforting comment was, "Don't worry, be happy — I have covered your one bid." He leaned back with a big grin on his face. North was careful to dump the Jack of diamonds on the first trick and South played the nine — a truly magnificent discard. Now East shifted to a small trump and South immediately cleared the suit by playing his three top winners. The King of diamonds was cashed and the deuce was placed on the table. East was buried alive with all good red cards as he easily reached 10 bags and dropped 100 points. The grin became an expression of absolute shock. It was a bad day for science! On the next hand North/South ended the game and East grumbled about how unlucky he was. These are the quirks which occasionally appear and you have to be prepared. East really played like a "drib" as he should have discarded the diamond ten on trick one, ruffed the expected club return (by his partner), and taken his top red suit winners, as in the text. The diamond Queen is led, and South has no defense. If South grabbed the King, East would be out of the lead; if he ducked, East would have escaped with a low spade. Note: if South could see his partner's hand, he would lead a low club for a heart return!!

HAND 4- "MAMA SAID THERE'LL BE DAYS LIKE THIS"

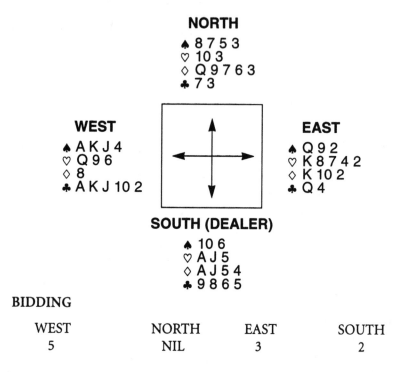

NORTH
♠ 8 7 5 3
♡ 10 3
◊ Q 9 7 6 3
♣ 7 3

WEST
♠ A K J 4
♡ Q 9 6
◊ 8
♣ A K J 10 2

EAST
♠ Q 9 2
♡ K 8 7 4 2
◊ K 10 2
♣ Q 4

SOUTH (DEALER)
♠ 10 6
♡ A J 5
◊ A J 5 4
♣ 9 8 6 5

BIDDING

WEST	NORTH	EAST	SOUTH
5	NIL	3	2

This is a classic example of what appears to be a sound nil bid; however, the spade length is a bit suspect. North/South were losing by 150 points and their situation was desperate. We still would recommend this nil bid anyway as partner probably could help with one spade honor and the other spades could be used for underruffing. The opening lead was the Queen of clubs, followed by the nine, King and seven. Now the eight of diamonds was pushed. North played the seven, East covered with the King, and South ducked, saving the Ace for nil protection. East trotted out the ten of diamonds and South inserted the Ace as West trumped with the Jack and north dumped his Queen of diamonds. A small spade was played by West to his partner's Queen and another diamond was returned. South covered with the Jack and West trumped with the Ace of spades. The King of spades was cashed, as East played the nine. The Queen of hearts was led, North played the ten, East played the eight and South played low. The nine of hearts was played, North dropped the three, East played the seven and South took the Jack. Everything looked fine except for one small detail. North had two trumps remaining, East had one and the nil was doomed. This is just one of those unfortunate situations which does occur and is comparable to a "fix" in bridge. Basically, your play is correct, yet the results are unfavorable due to the distribution of the cards and power of the trump suit. We will observe an extreme example of this theme later on in this book.

HAND 5 -"EVERY MAN FOR HIMSELF"

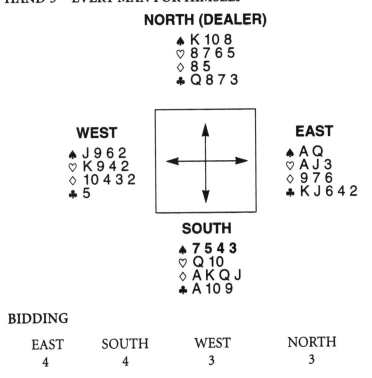

NORTH (DEALER)
♠ K 10 8
♡ 8 7 6 5
◊ 8 5
♣ Q 8 7 3

WEST
♠ J 9 6 2
♡ K 9 4 2
◊ 10 4 3 2
♣ 5

EAST
♠ A Q
♡ A J 3
◊ 9 7 6
♣ K J 6 4 2

SOUTH
♠ 7 5 4 3
♡ Q 10
◊ A K Q J
♣ A 10 9

BIDDING

EAST	SOUTH	WEST	NORTH
4	4	3	3

It was another close game and the score was tied at 430 apiece. Bags were not a factor. South, who might have conservatively bid three, felt compelled to bid four in order to avoid losing by 10 points. However, this created this somewhat peculiar situation of both sides bidding seven! The total of 14 tricks condemned someone to failure and so it became a ferocious battle. Incidentally, this is the type of hand that you would see in the variation of spades referred to as "homicide." The total number of tricks in the homicide variation must equal 14 and the final bidder is required to ensure that total. We need to review two of the bids. West was somewhat aggressive as he hoped to score his King of hearts and two trump. North was very aggressive as he hoped to score his Queen of clubs and two trump. East's bid is very reasonable and South had a good shot at fulfilling his as well, especially with the extra spade and three top tricks. West opened an obvious five of clubs, North played low and East's Jack (a wonderfully imaginative finesse) was taken by the Ace. South now started the diamond suit and was pleased to take three rounds as his partner discarded a heart on the third round. Having fulfilled his bid, South now continued with a fourth round of diamonds and his partner could not resist trumping with the eight (a very odd play), as East took his Queen of spades. The Ace of spades was cashed with everyone following, as West was quite pleased to see the ten drop. East paused to take the King of clubs as West played a low heart. Now the Ace of hearts was dropped on the table, followed by a small heart to the King. A low spade was returned to North's King. The critical junction was reached. Each side had five tricks. North now tried a heart. East's Jack was trumped by South, and the last two tricks were scored by the Jack and nine of trump. The final result was East/West seven tricks; North/South six tricks (and defeat). We really have to appreciate the absolutely brilliant play of the Jack of clubs on the first trick. How could East have known the importance of this play? This was truly a memorable hand.

Chapter Thirteen

UNCLE JOE'S HOT TIPS
A BAKER'S DOZEN

I   BIDDING

1. Your bid is influenced by your opponents' bid, your part-
    ner's bid and the score of the game. Gauge the strength of
    your hand accordingly.

2. It is better to bid slightly conservatively rather than risk
    defeat by over-aggressively bidding.

3. The longer a suit is, the less number of tricks you can
    expect to take. Do not overvalue lengthy suits or suits with
    separated honor cards.

4. Do not bid nil if you have more than one prospective loser
    or separate high trump. An unusually high bid by your
    partner or your opponents may give you some flexibility.

II PLAY OF THE HAND

5. Rarely take a trick from your partner unless you have a good reason for doing so.
6. If your partner has bid nil, it is absolutely essential to save your high cards or high spades for the latter stages of the hand (you may have to protect him at a critical time).
7. "Second hand low" is generally good advice, as it gives your partner a chance to win a trick. "Third hand high" is also proper as it prevents the last player from winning a trick cheaply. Note: The exception to third hand high is forcing the opponents' to take bags.
8. Lead trump as often as possible if you want to set up a solid side suit. This is called "flushing."

III DEFENSE

9. The best defense against an opponent's nil bid is the repeated lead of low cards in the side suits — hoping to flush out an Ace or King. Another good strategy is to drain trump from the partner of the nil bidder by leading middle or low spades.
10. Watch your partner's discards and look for encouraging high card signals or discouraging low card signals.
11. Never lead a suit in which both opponents are void. This is called a "ruff-sluff."
12. A safe lead is the top of a sequence (K Q J). A poor play is the underlead of an unprotected honor card or the underlead of an Ace. This may give away a "free finesse."
13. Watch those bags! Once again do not take excess bags in order to set low level bids of less than four.

ETHICS AND COURTESY

It is very important to remember that Spades is only a game and should have no bearing on the real world. You should be polite and courteous with both your partner and your opponents. If your partner succeeds in his bid, a few words of encouragement will go a long way. If your partner makes an error, be understanding and sympathetic.

After all, you might make a mistake during the next hand. No one likes to be criticized, berated or insulted. Repeated displays of sarcasm, bragging, and abusive behavior will result in your playing against computers or by yourself. At times it may be frustrating to lose, but in Spades, as in life, that is the way it goes. Finally, it is a very good idea to find a partner with whom you can play on a regular basis. This will help you to improve your game and develop a rapport. It is a lot more fun to be both competitive and gracious. Remember we all start out as beginners.

Chapter Fourteen

THE FINAL HANDS

A "THE OPTICAL ILLUSION"

NORTH
♠ 4
♡ A Q 8 4 3
◊ A 10 7 6 3
♣ J 9

WEST	EAST
♠ A Q J 9 5	♠ K 10 8 7 6
♡ VOID	♡ J 10 9 6
◊ K J 9 8	◊ VOID
♣ Q 10 8 7	♣ A K 3 2

SOUTH (DEALER)
♠ 3 2
♡ K 7 5 2
◊ J 5 4 2
♣ 6 5 2

BIDDING

WEST	NORTH	EAST	SOUTH
5	2	5	NIL

This is the most incredible deal you will ever see. It occurred in a tournament game on the Internet. I have never seen this happen! This is a hand which will probably appear once every 100 years. The bidding appears to be reasonable and South's nil looks quite solid. East led the three of clubs as he took an immediate shot at breaking the nil. South played the deuce, and West took the Queen. West now returned a club to East's Ace. East played the Jack of hearts, South played low and West trumped with the five. Now West played the eight of diamonds and North played the ten while East ruffed. North made the comment, "Oh my God," as he realized what was going on. East now returned another heart, South played the King and West ruffed with the nine, figuring North probably had the Ace. A diamond was returned as East trumped. Back and forth they went as they took eight ruffs SEPARATELY. West now cashed the Ace of spades, felling his partner's King. This left the deuce of spades as the only remaining spade. Amazingly enough, South was forced to take a trick with this lowly card. This was truly an incredible result. Surely it was a once in a lifetime occurrence. I wonder how many people could have possibly figured that South would lose his nil to the deuce of spades, especially considering all of the trump strength amassed in both opponent's hands. I guess it goes to show you that you never can tell what the Card Gods have in store for you.

B "MAGIC"

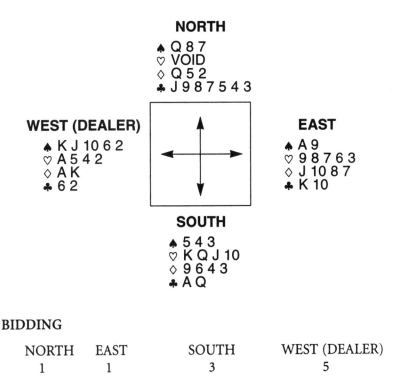

NORTH
♠ Q 8 7
♡ VOID
◇ Q 5 2
♣ J 9 8 7 5 4 3

WEST (DEALER)
♠ K J 10 6 2
♡ A 5 4 2
◇ A K
♣ 6 2

EAST
♠ A 9
♡ 9 8 7 6 3
◇ J 10 8 7
♣ K 10

SOUTH
♠ 5 4 3
♡ K Q J 10
◇ 9 6 4 3
♣ A Q

BIDDING

NORTH	EAST	SOUTH	WEST (DEALER)
1	1	3	5

Another "dogfight" was at hand, and North/South were trailing by a score of 440 to 390. Each side had two bags — no problem here! The bidding appeared to be normal, as North feared a trump loser (otherwise a nil was a consideration). East tossed in a conservative one, South counted three winners and trotted out an ambitious three bid. West grabbed at the five bid — he saw at least two trump tricks as well as three red suit winners — and the score of 60 seemed to go along nicely with the 440 already on the board. Anyone looking at the West hand would agree that five tricks were a lead-pipe cinch! West knew his partner could be counted on for one trick. All of the campers were happy. Now it was time for magic!

South (on lead) led the top of his heart sequence. It was a perfectly normal choice; but the Card Gods were about to take over! West hesitated, and finally flew with his Ace. The low spade ruff by North sent a jolt through West! The best was yet to come! North shifted to a low club, and East hesitated before dropping his ten. South read the "hitch" as a club problem (East probably had the King), and his insight proved to be quite correct as he played the club Queen, and the finesse worked. Now the Queen-Jack-ten of hearts were cashed, as East and West helplessly followed suit and North unloaded his three diamonds. South led the diamond three, and poor West watched his Ace get ruffed away! Another club to South's Ace was followed by a diamond lead and another ruff by North. The big "wood" had been felled from the West hand!

By this time, North/South had taken the first EIGHT tricks and the opponents' contract of six was in the tank! The remainder of the hand was cheerfully conceded, and the East/West score dropped by sixty points. The game ended after the next deal.

Was it "Magic"? Was it "Serendipity"? How about "Intuition"? I leave that up to you. All I know is that I had another hand for the book! You just don't see "ruffing finesses" everyday! A rare bird — indeed!

Chapter Fifteen

THE LAWS OF SPADES CONDENSED

Until now, the game of Spades has had no proper set of Laws. We do realize that there are a plethora of variations and interpretation of rules. This book will identify The Official General Laws of Spades for the Standard Four Partnership Game. The advanced book will further establish laws and rules for all related forms of the game and variations.

1. THE PACK

The game of Spades is played with a standard deck of 52 cards and back design, and consisting of 13 cards in each of four suits. The cards in each suit rank downward from the Ace (highest) to the deuce (lowest). The spade suit is designated as trump (outstanding or highest for each hand).

2. NUMBER OF PLAYERS

Three or four may play. There is a two player version referred to as "honeymoon" and the three player version called "individuals or singles." The best game, standard for parties and tournaments is four-handed featuring partners. Each partnership consists of two players seated opposite each other. Partners may be determined by previous arrangement or by drawing cards. Note: *Advanced Play and Strategy* will review the two- and three-players games, as well as the multiple variations.

3. THE SHUFFLE, CUT AND DEAL

These are standard procedural aspects and have been reviewed previously. Note — two decks are suggested for each table — with one deck in play while the other deck is prepared for the next deal.

4. OBJECT OF THE GAME

The object of the game is to win tricks in quantity to fulfill bid contracts. Points are credited for making contracts and nil bids. A small premium (usually one point each) is also awarded for overtricks. Points are deducted for unsuccessful (set) contracts as well as accumulation of increments of ten overtricks (referred to as "bags"). The game limit for the standard partnership variation is 500 points; the game limit for individuals is 300 points. There is also a negative limit of minus 300 points.

5. OPENING BID/OPENING LEAD

The opening bid is made by the player sitting to the immediate left of the dealer. The opening lead is made by the player seated to the right of the dealer. Note — An alternate variation is to have the person seated to the left hand of the dealer open the round of bidding AND make the opening lead. In either case, this needs to be agreeable to all four players. Another variation is the opening lead of the deuce of clubs and the winner of this trick leads to trick 2. The deal rotates for every hand. There is only one round of bidding and bids are identified by the word nil indicating zero tricks. Blind nil, also indicates zero tricks, and must be made without seeing your cards. There is an option to pass cards (between partners) after a blind nil bid. This must be agreeable to all players at the table. All other bids are stated with a number from 1–13. Suits and no trump are not mentioned. Whoever makes the opening lead must place a card face up on the table; spades may not be led until the trump suit has been discarded or the player on lead has nothing but spades.

6. THE PLAY

After the opening lead, each player in clockwise turn, plays a card and the four cards as played constitute a trick. A player must follow suit if possible. This takes precedence over any other requirement. The player who wins a trick, leads to the next trick. If unable to follow suit, a player may play any card which is called a "discard." He also has the option to play a spade which is called "trumping." Any card that is played by placing it face up on the table is determined as "boarded." If such a card is visible to any player or is played in a manner that clearly indicates an intention to play this card, constitutes a completed action. ("A card seen is a card played.") If a player leads out of turn, he is required to place this card on the table and must play it at the next legal opportunity (penalty card). The director is called if this occurs in a tournament.

7. THE REVOKE (RENEGE)

If a player discards when able to follow suit, he is said to renounce. There is no penalty if he corrects his renounce before any card is played to the next trick. However, if the trick involving the renounce is completed and a card has been played to the next trick, the renounce becomes a revoke. The penalty for an established revoke is two tricks or loss of bid against the offender; however, a director must be called in order to establish culpability and make a final ruling. If it is determined that a revoke was intentional to avoid taking unwanted tricks, the director may assess a penalty of five bags or loss of bid.

8. CLAIMS AND CONCESSONS

If a player exposes his hand and claims all remaining tricks he must announce the order of his plays. If he fails to announce the order of his plays any other player may direct how he played his cards. In any case, the director needs to be consulted to make the final ruling. If a player exposes only one card prematurely, this card is deemed to be a lead out of turn and that card must remain on the table and played at next legal opportunity.

9. IRREGULARITIES

If any player calls attention to an irregularity, the director should be called at once. If the offender attempts to correct his irregularity he may be further penalized. If two players play a card simultaneously to a trick, the second player is deemed to be in his proper turn. The winner of each trick collects his four cards into a neat packet and lays it face down in front of himself. After the last trick has been played and collected, the North player may ask each player who won any trick for verification. If there are any other questions, the director must be called.

10. TABLE TALKING, MANNERISMS, GESTURES, HESITATIONS DURING THE PLAY OF HAND, AND ALL OTHER FORMS OF INAPPROPRIATE BEHAVIOR ARE UNACCEPTABLE. EACH PLAYER IS ASKED TO PLAY COURTEOUSLY AND ETHICALLY.

11. The International Hearts and Spade Players' Association (IHSPA) reserves the right to further amend and update these laws.

Chapter Sixteen

DUPLICATE SPADES
STRATEGY AND TECHNIQUE

Duplicate is a format which has been successfully used by the American Contract Bridge League (ACBL) for several years. The purpose of Duplicate is to eliminate the luck of the deal and to **compare your skill to other players holding the same cards.** In this way, the strength of each **partnership can be accurately determined. There are two movements — Individuals and Partners.** We will be discussing the Partnership variation.

Each hand is a **separate entity,** and unlike a standard game of 10 deals or 500 points, Duplicate is structured on a complete Round or Match of a **pre-determined number of deals,** or hands. A typical Tournament usually features 28 or 32 deals. You will be assigned a pair number and Direction (North/South or East/West). After which you will proceed to your First Round Table. A round consists of three or four hands. At the end of the round, you will move to the next highest numbered table if you are an East/West pair. North/South pairs remain stationery at their respective tables. Now the play begins!

This is accomplished by the use of a **duplicate board** which, in effect, is a plastic holder for cards. Each board contains **one complete**

deal. The deal is separated into four hands, one for each player. Partners still play as a team and sit opposite from each other. The number, direction and opening bidder are clearly identified. In Duplicate Spades, the **left hand opponent** of the dealer has the **opening bid** and the **first lead** is made by the player to the dealers' immediate **right.** Each board holds a hand record sheet, which allows the verification of a hand to be accomplished easily. There is also a **traveling score** which identifies every contract, final score, number of tricks, and bags taken. Although the bidding is still accomplished in one round, the play of the hand is different. Normally, the cards in a typical "fresh deal game" are thrown into the middle of the table, and the winner of each trick gathers up the four cards (a book) and places them in front of himself. In Duplicate, the big difference in the routine is the play of the hand. Instead of tossing the cards into the middle of the table, you simply **turn up each card in front of you.** If your side wins a trick, your card is then turned over vertically. If your side loses a trick your card is turned horizontally. This facilitates the tracking of all tricks when the hand is over and is very easy to determine the number of tricks taken by each side. If a nil bidder takes a trick, this can be identified quite quickly. The North player is the scorer. The **final score for both partnerships** is recorded on the traveling score sheet and then the hand record sheet is quickly checked to determine that the right cards are returned to each pocket. It is always a good idea to double check the scores before the score sheet is returned to the Board. Both forms are then folded and carefully placed in the North pocket of the board (on top of the hand).

Accurate bidding and play is rewarded with a good score. If you underbid, you will be hurt by bags and a lower score. Overbidding will result in frequent "sets" or defeated contracts. If all pairs bid and make the **same** score, then the board is a "wash," and everyone receives an **average score.** If your team has the **best score** for the board, your side earns a **"top,"** which is terrific! Remember, your performance for each hand is compared to the other pairs in the **same direction** who also played the **same hands!** Nils are always a premium. At the end of the session, the scores are then tallied, board by board. The method of comparison is called **"match pointing"** — each hand is a separate entity. Thus, a poor result on one hand can be easily offset by a good result on another. **There are two winners (pairs) for each session.**

North/South and East/West produce a representative winner for their Direction(s). This adjusted playoff then matches those two winning partnerships against each other in one final fresh deal game. The **Director** is the person responsible for the event, and for making any rulings which may become necessary. He or she is there to help and guide.

You will like Duplicate — as it allows you to see exactly how well you do against other players. While the luck of the deal is eliminated, you still have to make the most of the cards you are holding. It is the measuring standard for Bridge, and now Spades can move into a new "era" as well! Someday, Duplicate Spades Clubs will be accessible on a local basis. As of this writing, Duplicate is available only at national tournaments. Look for announcements in the newsletter of the International Hearts and Spades Players' Association (IHSPA).

Chapter Seventeen

SPADES AND THE INTERNET

The increased popularity of the Internet has certainly expanded the horizons of card players everywhere.

Now any player with a computer (and modem) can play a good game of Spades with quality opponents. All ranges of skills are represented at various sites. Most of the Classic Card Games, including Spades, are free — although it is best to look at the regulations, fee schedules (if any), and terms of access. Technology is constantly changing, and most sites are improving all of the time. Listed below are three of the best Internet sites for the game of Spades.

1. MICROSOFT INTERNET GAMING ZONE

(www.zone.com)

This is the Premier Site on the Internet. The Classic Card Games are first-rate, and best of all — are free! Graphics are superb, and the Spades Rooms are very accessible. The cards are easy to read, and the score is automatically maintained. You can chat with your opponents, or if you want to watch a game, there is the "kibitz" option. There is a multiplicity of tiers from beginner through expert. Rooms are categorized by level of skill. There is also a Ratings System, which allows any player to gauge his or her strength by playing against opponents of comparable or greater rank. Several dedicated Hosts, Tourney Directors, and Systems Operators (Sysops) help to maintain order, and keep things moving smoothly. There is a full information Center in the Lobby with Game Tips, Tournament Listings, News, a Chat Room, a Monthly Column, and links to other sites. A neat system for sending messages to other Zone Members is also featured. This site pioneered the way for others. Registration is a one-time procedure, but you will be in the action within a few minutes! One of the more popular Spades events in the Zone may be found at this location—

www.geocities.com/colosseum/arena/3584

2.   TEN (Total Entertainment Network) Excite Home Games

(www.excite.com/play)

This is a nicely formatted site with an up-to-date design. You can play for free, and access is very easy. There are rooms for beginning, intermediate, and advanced players. Rules and levels are clearly outlined, and there is a Ratings area. One of the most outstanding features is the "customizing" option, where players can select the Rules for their game from a "menu" of choices. There is also a News column and informational listings. Plans to add additional games to the site are in the development stage. Spadeslovers of America (based in Missouri) conduct regularly scheduled events. This Site has a lot of potential, and is well worth exploring.

3.   M-PLAYER

(www.mplayer.com)

This very modern, really "hip" location with some of the fanciest graphics and design features you will ever see reminds me a bit of "M-TV" — with the spirit of the 90s in full bloom! Each player has the opportunity to select their own pictorial logo. The game of Spades is well represented, as are the other "Classic Card Games." You may play Spades for free, or participate in the optional "Plus" program.

MISCELLANEOUS:

Spades CDs:

Games CDs have been available for many years now. In the good old days of DOS and large "floppies," these were quite the rage! Modern CDs have come a long way! The opportunity to play against "artificial intelligence" is an alternative to the Internet game. Two of the best CDs featuring the game of Spades are:

1. Bicycle Hearts & Spades (Expert Software; Coral Gables, FL)
   This is one of many card games CDs produced by Expert Software, as part of the United States Playing Card Company's Series. It is designed for the Novice and Intermediate player. A really nice feature is the large sized-playing cards. You will recognize the famous "Bicycle" logo. The instructions are very simple, and the standard rules for both games are followed. An update for this product is scheduled for mid 1999.

2. Spades DeLuxe (Freeverse Software; NYC)
   Freeverse Software marketed Hearts Deluxe a few years ago, and now they have produced the Spades Deluxe Program. It will soon be ready for Windows and PC Systems; as of this writing, it is available only for Macintosh Computers. The range of play is from beginner to upper level Intermediate. A lot of creative programming went into the design of this product. The graphics are very clever, and the cute, thematic characters will impress everyone who uses this CD. Directions are easy to follow. For a good, competitive game with a "twist," I suggest that you check this out!

INTERNATIONAL HEARTS AND SPADES PLAYERS' ASSOCIATION (IHSPA)

For more detailed information about the IHSPA, I refer you to this site: (www.eccy.com). The Association is scheduled to launch in the first quarter of 1999, and will have a Delegate's meeting at the Hearts & Spades National Championships at Harrah's (Las Vegas) in the spring of 1999. Players will have the opportunity to earn a Life Master Award, and to play in sanctioned "live" events at various sites.

Good Luck in all of your Spades Endeavors!